MYSTERIOUS PLACES
THE LANDS OF THE BIBLE

MYSTERIOUS PLACES
THE LANDS
OF THE BIBLE

Philip Wilkinson & Jacqueline Dineen

Illustrations by Robert Ingpen

**DRAGON'S
WORLD**

Dragon's World Ltd
Limpsfield
Surrey RH8 0DY
Great Britain

First published by Dragon's World 1992

Simplified text and captions by **Jacqueline Dineen**
based on the *Encyclopedia of Mysterious Places*
by Robert Ingpen and Philip Wilkinson.

Editor	Diana Briscoe
Designer	Design 23
Art Director	Dave Allen
Editorial Director	Pippa Rubinstein

**British Library Cataloguing
in Publication Data**
The catalogue record for this book is
available from the British Library.

ISBN 1 80528 176 9

Printed in Italy

CONTENTS

General Introduction 10

Ur,
Iraq, c. 4000–2000 BC
13

✓ **Saqqara,**
Egypt, c. 2680 BC
21

Babylon,
Iraq, c. 1792–1750 BC and c. 625–540 BC
29

Boghazköy,
Turkey, c. 1700–1200 BC
37

✓ **Karnak,**
Egypt, c. 1480–1080 BC
45

✓ **Abu Simbel,**
Egypt, c. 1305–1220 BC
53

Khorsabad,
Iraq, 720–705 BC
59

Persepolis,
Iran, c. 520–330 BC
67

Petra,
Jordan, c. 170 BC–AD 100
77

✓ **Alexandria,**
Egypt, c. 320 BC–AD 391
83

Further Reading 91/Index 92

✓ = reviewed

Introduction

Today we know the Middle East as an area of great wealth, but also of violent conflict. It supplies much of the world's oil but is also the scene of many of the world's wars. This contrast has been the pattern in the area for thousands of years, for the Middle East has been the home of some of the world's richest and most successful empires.

The pharaohs of Egypt, for example, ruled their kingdom on the banks of the Nile for more than 2000 years. Although there were interruptions in their rule, their whole culture and lifestyle survived for the entire period. Other empires such as those of the Hittites (from what is now Turkey), Assyrians (from northern Iraq), and Persians (from Iran) did not last as long, but were highly successful in their day.

This part of the world is also familiar to many people because of the stories in the Bible. The Old Testament, especially, tells of events in the history of the Jews that also involve the other peoples that lived in the area. Perhaps the most famous examples are the stories about the relations between Israel and Egypt – the Egyptian domination of the Jews, and the episode called the Exodus when the Jews were said to have escaped from slavery in Egypt and returned to their own lands.

The splendours of the Bible lands

The peoples who have lived in the Middle East have left behind many remains of their civilisations – fortresses, palaces, temples and cities. Such places give us a glimpse of their builders' sophistication and power. Some of the remains, like those of the great Hittite fortress at Boghazköy, Turkey, are now in such a state of ruin that it is difficult to tell what they were originally like. Others, such as some of the temples and pyramids in Egypt are very well preserved.

But all these places have their mysteries. Who built them and why? How were they used? What ceremonies took place in the palaces and what rituals in the temples? What were the people who built them really like? How did they live their lives? This book answers questions like these about the mysterious places of the Bible lands.

The cradle of civilisation

This area is interesting for another reason. It was here that civilisation as we know it really began. In the fertile lands near the Rivers Tigris and Euphrates many thousands of years ago, people started farming. They realised that this was a more efficient way of obtaining food than the hunting and gathering that they had used before – in fact they could produce more food than they needed.

This food surplus meant that not everyone had to be employed producing food – some could become specialist craft workers, perhaps making pots or tools that they could trade for food. It also meant that people could congregate together and live in towns – something that had not happened before. Some of these towns grew into the first cities, the centres of power and civilisation in the Middle East.

This book includes some of the earliest cities, Ur and Babylon in Mesopotamia, the land between the Tigris and Euphrates. It looks at the long-lived civilisation of Egypt, particularly the unique step pyramid at Saqqara and two very different temples at Karnak and Abu Simbel.

Then there are sites that typify the world of the later Middle Eastern empires: the Hittite fortress of Boghazköy, the Assyrian royal city of Khorsabad, and the palace of the Persian kings at Persepolis.

Finally the book shows what happened to the area later, under the influence of ancient Greece. Alexandria, a city of culture and learning in Egypt, and Petra, an amazing town with buildings cut out of the pink-coloured red cliffs, complete the picture. Petra in particular, lost among the hills of Jordan and isolated from outsiders until it was 'rediscovered' in the nineteenth century, sums up the mystery and fascination of this part of the world.

Philip Wilkinson

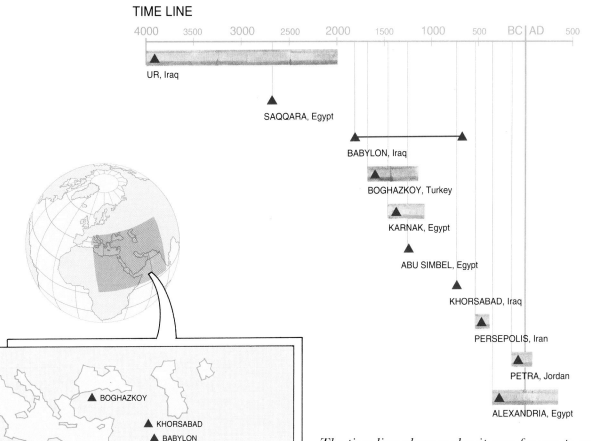

TIME LINE

4000   3500   3000   2500   2000   1500   1000   500   BC | AD   500

UR, Iraq

SAQQARA, Egypt

BABYLON, Iraq

BOGHAZKOY, Turkey

KARNAK, Egypt

ABU SIMBEL, Egypt

KHORSABAD, Iraq

PERSEPOLIS, Iran

PETRA, Jordan

ALEXANDRIA, Egypt

BOGHAZKOY
KHORSABAD
BABYLON
ALEXANDRIA   PETRA   UR   PERSEPOLIS
SAQQARA
KARNAK
ABU SIMBEL

The time line above makes it easy for you to see at a glance which civilisations in this book came first and which came later. Along the top of the line are dates; you can tell from the length of the bars below how long or short a time the site was important. Look at the map to see where the sites are in relation to each other.

11

Ur

Iraq, c.4000–2000 BC

An ancient Sumerian city and site of a magnificent ziggurat.
Who were the people who gave us the
world's first literature yet carried out strange and sinister royal burials?

About 7500 years ago groups of nomads began to settle in the fertile valley between the Tigris and Euphrates rivers, in what is now Iraq. This land was called Sumer or Mesopotamia. The people who settled there gradually developed an organised civilisation. They learned to write and gave the world its first literature. They also built some of the great cities of ancient times. One of the most remarkable of these cities was Ur.

The Bible tells us about Ur. According to the book of Genesis, it was built by the ancestors of Abraham who wanted 'to build a city, and a tower, whose top may reach unto heaven'.

The same but different

The Sumerians did not build only one city. Sumer was divided into independent city-states and each city had its own ruler and way of life. But all the cities of the Sumerian civilisation had some things in common. The people all spoke the same language and had the same way of writing. They also had similar methods of trading and everyone had a common religion. Every city had a temple to the gods. These temples were stepped pyramids called ziggurats.

We can piece together the history of Ur from the Bible and also from the written records the Sumerians left behind. Archaeologists have uncovered remains which help us to imagine what Ur looked like. It was one of the largest cities in Mesopotamia and it had the finest ziggurat.

Fighting for power

Sometimes the city-states fought with each other, and one ruler would become more powerful than the others for a time. Ur seems to have had two important periods in its history. The first began in about

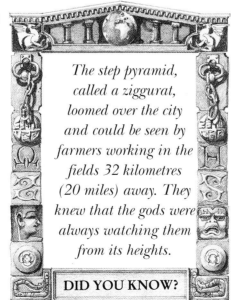

The step pyramid, called a ziggurat, loomed over the city and could be seen by farmers working in the fields 32 kilometres (20 miles) away. They knew that the gods were always watching them from its heights.

DID YOU KNOW?

The streets of Ur were bustling with people and animals. Behind the mud brick houses stood the huge ziggurat. The clay tablet at the top gives an example of the Sumerian wedge-shaped script.

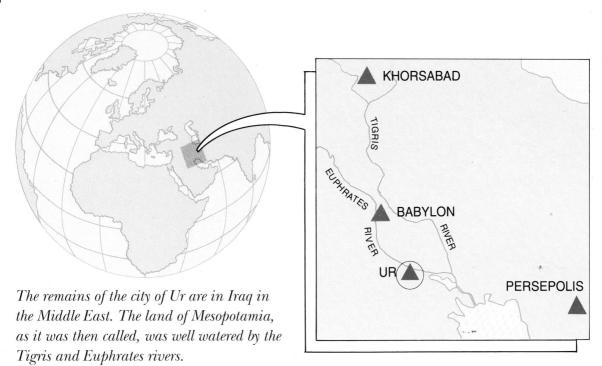

The remains of the city of Ur are in Iraq in the Middle East. The land of Mesopotamia, as it was then called, was well watered by the Tigris and Euphrates rivers.

2800 BC. Archaeologists have found a huge royal burial ground with thousands of tombs from this period.

The grave goods (things buried with the dead person) found in the tombs tell us something about the people who lived in Ur at the time. They were buried with the tools of their trade, weapons, vessels and ornaments. Kings and queens had jewellery and elaborate headdresses. We can see from the precious stones and metals that this was a time of power and wealth for the city.

Conquered by Akkad

This period ended in 2300 BC when the Sumerians were conquered by Sargon, leader of the Akkadians who lived to the north of Sumer.

Sargon was the world's first empire-builder. He made Akkad and Sumer into one big kingdom, and then conquered northern Mesopotamia and Anatolia (modern Turkey).

Sargon ruled over his kingdom for fifty-six years but after his death it was raided by a mountain people, the Gutians. Sargon's great empire gradually collapsed and by about 2100, the Sumerians had regained their power. This was the beginning of Ur's second important period in history.

Power and glory

The Sumerians had a number of great leaders at this time, but the finest was a king called Ur-Nammu. The splendid ziggurat at Ur was built during his reign.

The city also started to grow much larger at about this time. We are not sure why this happened but it was probably to do with its advantageous position on the banks of the Euphrates River. There was good land and water for growing food. The early settlers all farmed the land and grew just enough food for themselves, but in time farmers could grow enough to feed other people as well.

This meant that some people could leave the land and turn their hands to other things, such as becoming craftsmen, builders and scribes (the people who kept the written records). The city's prosperity probably encouraged more people to move there, and so it continued to grow.

Hot line to the gods

We know from written records that the Sumerians worshipped more than 2000 different gods. Why were there so many? One reason is that each citizen chose a personal god who would look after him and put his point of view to the main gods.

The most important Sumerian god was the moon god, Nanna. Small moons made of copper have been found at the ziggurat of Ur, which show that Nanna and his wife, Ningal, were worshipped there.

Writing in clay

The Sumerians wrote on clay tablets using an alphabet using cuniform (see page 19) and many of these have been found in excavations of Ur. Some of these tablets tell us about farming. We know that the Sumerians grew cereal crops such as barley, and kept cattle.

There are tablets about the jobs people did in the city – bricklayers, carpenters, metal-workers, cooks and doctors are all mentioned.

A schoolboy in Ur

The Sumerians had schools and one tablet gives a surprisingly familiar account of a school day. A schoolboy runs to school because he knows he will be caned if he is late. He recites work he has learned from his tablet and writes out a new tablet. We learn that children were beaten for talking, standing up in class or poor copying.

The Sumerians lost their power in about 2000 BC when neighbouring peoples conquered them, but the tablets they wrote were passed on and stored in libraries. That is how we know so much about the Sumerians.

Ur-Nammu

Ur-Nammu ruled over a large kingdom from his capital cities of Ur and Uruk. This included the land between the lower Tigris and Euphrates rivers, the city of Assur further up the Tigris, and the city of Susa, now in Iran. The king controlled his people by dividing the kingdom up into about forty districts. Each district had its own governor who reported directly to the king.

As the kingdom grew bigger, Ur-Nammu became very wealthy and used his wealth to rebuild his capital cities. There was no stone on the plains of Sumer, so the people used mud bricks which they baked hard in the sun. These bricks were not strong enough to stand up to the hot sunshine plus seasons of heavy rain. The buildings often collapsed in wet weather. Ur-Nammu wanted his buildings to last longer without needing repair, so he used bricks which were fired in a kiln to make them harder and stronger.

An early king of Ur.

The Ziggurat of Ur

The Bible talks about a tower, but a ziggurat was actually shaped like a pyramid. The walls did not slope in a smooth line, like the pyramids in Egypt but were built in a series of steps or terraces. The ziggurat was supposed to bring the priests nearer to heaven, as though they were standing on a mountain.

The ziggurat of Ur was one of the world's first 'temple-mountains'. It was built in the holy part of the city, the temenos, near Ur-Nammu's palace. The ruins of the ziggurat are still standing, 4000 years after it was built. They look impressive even today, so we can imagine how spectacular the complete building must have been. The base of the ziggurat measured 63 x 43 metres (207 x 141 ft) at the bottom and it was about 30 metres (100 ft) high.

This may not seem very tall when you compare

it with some modern buildings, but it is incredible when you think that the whole ziggurat was built with small bricks. Armies of workers were needed to build it and keep it in good repair.

The ziggurat had three terraces, and the walls were sloped to make the temple look even more like a mountain. The terraces were reached by a triple staircase. At the top was the sanctuary building, where the gods lived and where food and wine were offered to them by the priests.

The ziggurat looks like a building you can go into, but in fact it is a solid block of mud bricks with a layer of stronger, kiln-fired bricks on the outside. The sanctuary was the only part people could enter. Most of the outer bricks are stamped with the name of Ur-Nammu but some have the name of later rulers. So even these tougher bricks needed to be replaced at times.

Royal burial and suicides

When the archaeologist Sir Leonard Woolley excavated the royal burial ground at Ur, he discovered a strange thing. When Sumerian kings and queens died, their courtiers and servants were buried with them. Some kings had as many as eighty servants in their tombs. Each body had a cup near it, which led Woolley to believe that the servants had taken poison in the tomb.

Woolley began to piece together this mysterious and sinister burial ritual. First the ruler was placed in the tomb. Then three or four chosen attendants were buried with him and took their poison. The inner tomb was sealed up with mud bricks and plaster. Next, a great funeral procession entered the outer chamber of the tomb. First came the ladies of the court dressed in all their finery. Musicians played harps and servants led ox-carts filled with offerings. The humblest servants followed behind.

An example of the royal headdresses found in the tombs at Ur.

Harp from a royal burial.

They would all go into the tomb and take their poison. The tomb was then sealed up, while the rest of the people held a funeral feast outside.

Sir Leonard Woolley and Ur

The British archaeologist, Sir Leonard Woolley, was the first and most famous excavator of the city of Ur. He began work there in 1922 and discovered the royal burial ground in 1923. Woolley wrote popular accounts of his work and the evidence he had discovered. These started a wave of interest in the archaeology of the Bible lands.

Woolley made some amazing finds. In the royal tombs he uncovered delicate gold and silver jewellery and headdresses, gold and silver vessels and ornaments, and a gold helmet engraved to look like a wig. His summaries, as he pieced together the facts, painted a vivid but rather gruesome picture of the funeral rituals.

Visitors to Ur today can see the ruins of the ziggurat and parts of the foundations of houses and other buildings.

Trading patterns

The city-states were in an excellent position for trading because goods could be transported along the rivers, particularly the Euphrates. The jewellery and ornaments found in the royal burial ground show that the Sumerians were skilled craftworkers in metal and precious stones. They could import the raw materials they needed and sell the goods they made.

The people kept written records about trade. We know from clay tablets found at Ur that semi-precious stones such as lapis lazuli and carnelian came to Ur from Iran and Afghanistan and were used for making jewellery. Gold came from Anatolia (present-day Turkey) and silver from the Taurus mountains in southern Turkey. Cedar wood logs for building were floated along the Euphrates from Syria.

Pendant in the shape of a lion-headed eagle.

A clay tablet with cuneiform writing.

Personal seals with animals.

The birth of writing

The Sumerians developed a type of writing known as cuneiform (wedge-shaped) script. This is believed to be the oldest form of writing in the world. People used a stick, called a stylus, which had a triangle shape at the end. The stylus was pressed into soft clay to produce the marks that made up the script. The script was very complicated and consisted of 2000 different signs.

Each city had its scribes who studied hard to learn and perfect the script. At first, the scribes simply kept records about the city and the temple. As time went by, however, they began to write down the stories and poems which had been told by people for centuries. These stories had been handed down from one generation to the next by word of mouth. But when the scribes wrote them down, they became the world's first literature.

Saqqara
Egypt, c. 2680 BC

*The step pyramid at Saqqara was the world's
first stone monument and the first of Egypt's famous pyramids.
They were built to be the tombs of the pharaohs.*

Everyone has seen pictures of the pyramids of Egypt, even if they have not seen these incredible structures for themselves. They are some of the most famous 'wonders of the world'. Why did the ancient Egyptians choose to bury their pharaohs in such massive tombs? And how did they manage to build them without modern tools and machinery?

The most familiar pyramids stand on the banks of the Nile at Giza, but the strangest of all is probably the step pyramid at Saqqara, which is a bit further to the south-west. It was one of the world's earliest stone buildings and was the first Egyptian tomb to be built in this style.

Another interesting thing about Saqqara is that it does not look like the later pyramids. They have steeply sloping sides while Saqqara has six steps. It looks more like a Sumerian ziggurat than an Egyptian pyramid.

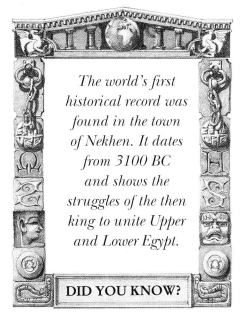

The world's first historical record was found in the town of Nekhen. It dates from 3100 BC and shows the struggles of the then king to unite Upper and Lower Egypt.

DID YOU KNOW?

A tomb fit for a king

Saqqara contains the tomb of Zoser, who was one of the first pharaohs of Egypt. Before his reign, nearly 5000 years ago, the nobility were buried in underground tombs called mastabas. The ancient Egyptians believed that when people died, they began a journey into another world. They buried their dead with many possessions and offerings to help them on their journey, so the tombs had to be large. But on the surface there was just a simple platform with sloping sides.

Zoser's tomb was built long before the king died. It was designed by Imhotep, who was a scribe and architect. Imhotep was so highly thought of in ancient Egypt that he was treated like a god. At first, Imhotep probably planned a mastaba for Zoser, but then his ideas began to change. He decided to add a low extension to the

*Armies of workers were needed to build a structure the size of Saqqara.
Here, blocks of stone are levered into place as the god-like figure of Imhotep looks on.
He is holding a square and a pendulum, the tools needed for pyramid building.*

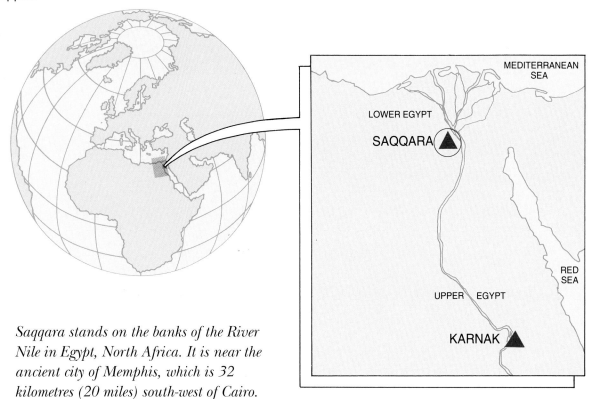

Saqqara stands on the banks of the River Nile in Egypt, North Africa. It is near the ancient city of Memphis, which is 32 kilometres (20 miles) south-west of Cairo.

platform on the surface, probably to make the tomb look more impressive. This would have given the monument two steps.

Once it was decided to change the original simple structure, ideas began to get even grander. If the tomb could have two steps, why could it not have four? And if it could have four, why not six platforms, each one smaller than the one below? So the idea of the pyramid was born.

You can take it with you!
The king's tomb did not stand alone. It was surrounded by a complex of chapels, courtyards and smaller tombs. The odd thing is that some of these buildings were false. You could not go inside because they were just solid blocks of brick covered with elaborate stonework. So why build them at all?

It is easier to understand this if we know what the ancient Egyptians

believed. They thought when people died and went to the next world, they needed everything they had needed on Earth. Everyone needed basic things like food and clothes but rich people took their worldly wealth as well.

A king was buried with thousands of pots and ornaments, furniture, jewellery and weapons. He needed servants but he did not take the real people like the rulers of Sumer. He was buried with wooden models of servants carrying out everyday tasks such as fishing and baking bread. So the false buildings round Zoser's tomb are models of buildings he would need in the afterlife.

Two of everything
Another mystery about Saqqara is that some of the buildings are in pairs. Surely Zoser would not need two chapels in the afterlife?

The explanation behind this puzzle is

that Egypt was divided into two parts, Upper and Lower Egypt, and the pharaohs were very powerful because they ruled over both. Wall paintings found in Egypt show pharaohs wearing double crowns as a symbol of the two Egypts (see page 26). We know from ancient Egyptian writings that coronations and other ceremonies contained rituals about being king of both parts. So the pairs of buildings are probably symbols of the same thing.

Fit to be king

One of the ceremonies which included a ritual about dual kingship was the royal jubilee. This was held when the king had been in power for some years. It was meant to give him new life and show that he had the strength to rule.

A carving on a wall at Saqqara shows the pharaoh running round the complex, perhaps to show that he was athletic and strong enough to be king. There was also a coronation ritual during which the king was crowned twice. He presented himself at a chapel for the gods of Upper Egypt and was then crowned king of Upper Egypt. Then he would go through the same ceremony for Lower Egypt.

When the king becomes a mummy

The ancient Egyptians believed that when people died they needed their bodies for the afterlife. So they preserved bodies by a long process called mummification.

Zoser's body would have been treated in this way before it was buried. The body was embalmed by covering it with a powder called natron. It was then wrapped in bandages soaked in oils. The face was covered with a mask which looked like the person's own face. Then the body was put into a shaped coffin. The coffin was put into a tomb filled with grave goods and statues.

People believed that the spirits of the dead could live in the statues, so they left food for them. The ceremony of offering food was carried out regularly.

Anubis, god of death

One of the many gods worshipped by the Egyptians was Anubis, the jackal-headed god of death. The jackal is a desert animal, and to the Egyptians the western desert was the home of the dead.

There are several stories about Anubis. One is that in early times he was god of death to the pharaoh. When a pharaoh had reigned for 28 years, Anubis appeared with a viper, which killed the king with its poison.

In other stories, Anubis is shown as the god of embalming, protecting the dead and preparing them for the next life. He often appears in paintings on the walls of tombs, doing this work.

Anubis, the jackal-headed god.

The Step Pyramid, Saqqara

Saqqara was the first monument to be built in stone and it was also the largest stone building anyone had attempted. By the time the later pyramids at Giza were built, people had learned how to haul huge blocks of stone, but the earlier builders could not do this, so Saqqara was built with fairly small blocks which could be levered into place. The pyramid and the group of buildings round it were unique at the time.

The pyramid is about 60 metres (200 ft) high and its base measures 125 x 109 metres (411 x 358 ft). It was built of gleaming white limestone which stood out against the surrounding countryside, so it made a striking landmark. Visitors to Saqqara must have marvelled at such a structure and thought it could only be built with the help of the gods.

In front of the pyramid was the courtyard,

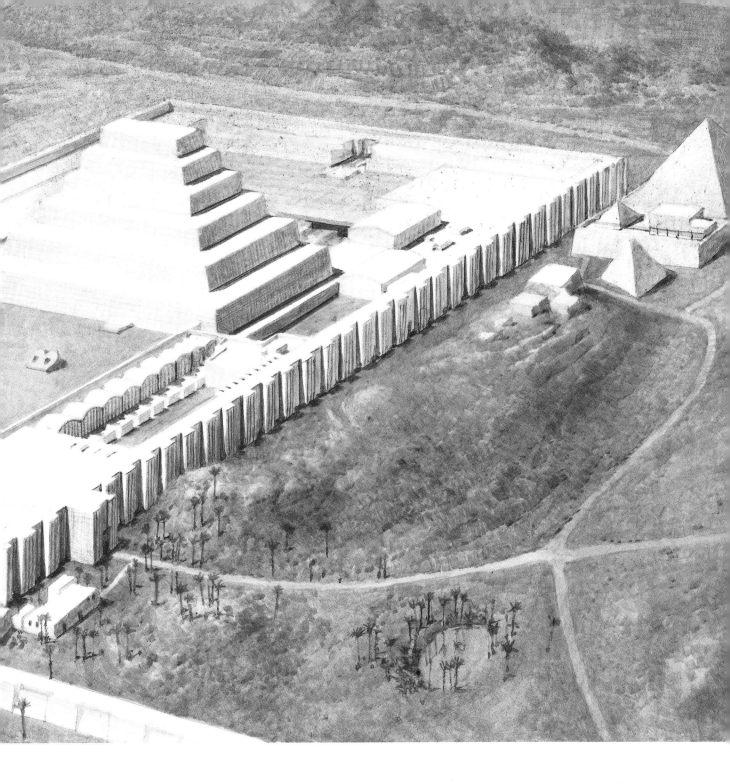

where the royal jubilee ceremonies were held. The pyramid was surrounded by chapels, courtyards and the king's temple. The whole complex of buildings was enclosed by a wall with fourteen gates carved into it. Only one of these gates was real. The rest were decoration.

One of Saqqara's mysteries is that there is a 'spare' tomb. Zoser was buried in the largest tomb and there are other tombs for members of the royal family. But there is also an empty tomb which is too small to hold a body. No one is sure why it was built.

The pyramid itself is a symbol of the king's power. The ancient Egyptians believed that the pharaoh represented the god Horus while he was alive and joined the sun-god Ra when he died. So the stepped pyramid may have been built as a staircase for the king to climb to the sun.

Imhotep and government

Egypt was one of the most successful early civilisations for two reasons. One was that it had an efficient system of government. The other was that the people held the pharaoh in high esteem because he gave them water for their land.

Without the River Nile, Egypt would be a desert. The pharaohs and their administrators developed an efficient irrigation system so that people could water the land and grow crops.

The administrators who kept the kingdom running smoothly were all scribes and they formed one of the most powerful groups in ancient Egypt.

Wall paintings show them doing a variety of jobs, such as counting the crops from a harvest and working out taxes which people had to pay to the pharaoh and his government. The taxes paid for structures like Saqqara, which were built by the people. But the people did not mind because to them the pharaoh was a god.

Imhotep was one of the most successful scribes. He was Zoser's

Farmers harvesting corn.

vizier or chief minister, which made him the most powerful man in the land, apart from the king. He became famous as a scribe, an astronomer, a writer, a doctor and an architect. He probably organised the vast armies of workers needed to build Saqqara. After his death, Imhotep was worshipped as the god of learning and medicine.

Upper and Lower Egypt

The Egyptian civilisation began in about 5000 BC when wandering hunters began to sow grain in the fertile soil on the banks of the Nile. They built villages and then towns and cities as the civilisation grew.

By about 3400 BC there were two separate kingdoms, Upper and Lower Egypt. Lower Egypt covered the region around the Nile delta, while Upper Egypt was governed from a town called Nekhen which was further south.

In 3200 BC Menes of Nekhen conquered the northern region and became the first king of both Egypts. From then on the two kingdoms were ruled by one king.

A pharaoh wearing the double crown of Egypt.

The water of life

The Nile flows through the whole of Egypt from north to south. Egypt has very little rain, so the river is the only means of supporting life there. The ancient Egyptians built all their cities by the river and farmed the land on its banks. Beyond these narrow strips of green lay the desert.

Until about thirty years ago when the Aswan Dam was built, the Nile flooded its banks every August. The floods spread silt as far as the edge of the desert. When the waters receded, the land was covered with fertile mud for planting crops.

The floods were useful but they could also be disastrous, as they sometimes destroyed towns along the river banks. At other times, there was not enough water to grow anything and there was a famine. The ancient Egyptians found ways of controlling the flood water by collecting it in basins along the banks. The water could then be taken to the fields when it was needed.

The Nile was also the main highway for transporting people and goods.

River boats carried people and goods.

Auguste Mariette

The first archaeologist to dig at Saqqara was a Frenchman called Auguste Mariette, born in 1821. Mariette began his career as an art teacher but was also an expert on ancient Egypt. In 1850 he gave up his teaching post and went to Egypt. His intention was to buy some manuscripts for the Louvre art gallery in Paris, but instead he began his excavations at Saqqara and other Egyptian sites. He has been condemned by Egyptians because he sent all his finds to Europe.

Mariette died in 1881 before he had finished his work at Saqqara, but his achievements aroused the interest of other archaeologists. Zoser's pyramid and the complex of buildings around it were excavated in the 1920s. Since then, many of the buildings have been rebuilt.

Babylon

Iraq, c. 1792–50 BC and c. 625–540 BC

*For centuries, people have told stories about the mystery and
magnificence of this ancient city – tales of great wealth mingled with evil.
But what do we really know about Babylon?*

Babylon, steeped in mysterious legends about gods and kings, sounds more like an imaginary city than a real place. But Babylon is very real. Like Ur, it was one of the ancient cities of Mesopotamia in the fertile valley between the Tigris and Euphrates Rivers.

Cimbing up to heaven

The Bible tells us two great stories about Babylon. The first, in the book of Genesis, is about the Tower of Babel, which the people started to build to reach Heaven. The story says that God saw that the people were getting big ideas and knew this would lead to trouble. He made people speak different languages so they could not understand each other and then he scattered them all over the world.

Archaeologists have found the remains of the ancient temple known as Babel which inspired this story.

The events in the second story happened over a thousand years later, in the reign of King Nebuchadnezzar. The Babylonians had conquered the Assyrians and taken control of their empire, which included Judah. Nebuchadnezzar captured thousands of Jews to work as slaves in Babylonia, and they were held captive in Babylon for many years.

A soldier king

These were the two periods in Babylon's history, when it dominated Mesopotamia. The story about the Tower of Babel is set during the reign of King Hammurabi (1792–50 BC). Babylon was one of several city-states in Mesopotamia which were struggling for power. When Hammurabi became ruler of Babylon, he conquered these warring city-states and brought them under his control. He put together

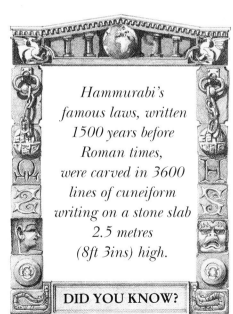

Hammurabi's famous laws, written 1500 years before Roman times, were carved in 3600 lines of cuneiform writing on a stone slab 2.5 metres (8ft 3ins) high.

DID YOU KNOW?

*The Tower of Babel may have been a ziggurat or it may have been a tall tower
like this one. We cannot be sure from the ruins. Here, slaves carry baskets
of fruit from the Hanging Gardens.*

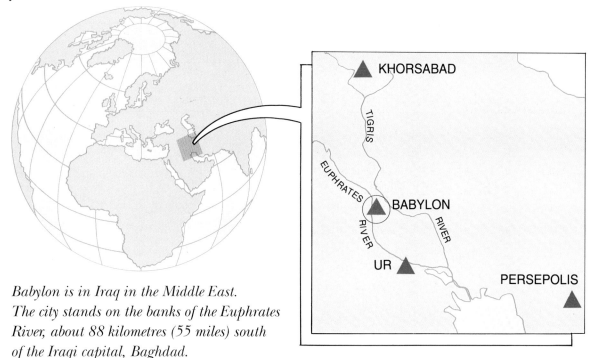

*Babylon is in Iraq in the Middle East.
The city stands on the banks of the Euphrates
River, about 88 kilometres (55 miles) south
of the Iraqi capital, Baghdad.*

one of history's first set of laws for the people of his kingdom to follow. Hammurabi also established one Babylonian religion and gave the priests more power.

Hammurabi's laws give us many clues about the people who lived in Babylon at the time. There seem to have been three separate groups or classes. Most people were 'free men', who were allowed to own houses and land and were protected by the laws. Free men ranged from farmers, craftsmen and merchants to the more powerful priests and government officials.

Below the free men was a group of people who had fewer rights. There are not so many clues about them, but they probably could not own property. They were not covered by the laws but came under the protection of the king. The lowest class of all consisted of slaves.

Hammurabi's Babylon

How and where did these people live? Unfortunately, the ruins of

Hammurabi's Babylon have long since been buried under newer buildings, so we have to guess what it looked like.

We can do this by comparing it with archaeological evidence in other great cities such as Ur. People would have lived in two-storey, mud-brick houses, built around a courtyard. The doors were probably made of reeds hung on a wooden frame. The temples where people worshipped their gods were probably ziggurats like Ur.

Babylon falls

During Hammurabi's reign, Babylon was a very rich city. It was the capital of the kingdom known as Babylonia which grew as Hammurabi conquered more lands. The kings who followed Hammurabi lost much of the territory he had won for them. The city became less important and less wealthy. It was invaded by powerful neighbours and its temples and palaces were destroyed.

Babylon did not dominate Mesopotamia again for more than a

thousand years. Then Nabopolassar (625–605 BC), came to the throne and won back the city's power.

The 'new' Babylon

Nabopolassar's main enemies were the Assyrians, who had built up a great empire and wanted to control Babylon. After years of fighting and scheming, Nabopolassar managed to overthrow the Assyrians. Their empire crumbled and Babylon became dominant again.

Nabopolassar began to rebuild the ruined city. When he died, his son, Nebuchadnezzar, came to the throne, and continued the work his father had begun. Nebuchadnezzar is well known because he enslaved the Jews, but he deserves to be remembered in other ways as well. He built temples, and magnificent palaces, a huge ziggurat, and surrounded the city with strong walls against invaders.

A cure for home sickness

Babylon's most famous and mysterious building, the Hanging Gardens, was also built during this period. The story goes that Nebuchadnezzar had the gardens made for his bride, Amitiya. She was the daughter of the king of the Medes, a land in what is now western Iran. Nebuchadnezzar thought the Hanging Gardens would remind Amitiya of the green and mountainous homeland she had left behind.

We know very little about the kings who followed Nebuchadnezzar, until 555 BC when Nabonidus came to the throne. He came from Harran in north-west Mesopotamia and we do not know why he became king of Babylon. He spent many years away from the city, leaving his son in charge. This was the start of Babylon's downfall. Eventually the city was conquered by the Persians under Cyrus the Great in 539 BC.

Marduk and his legend

The Babylonians worshipped many gods but their chief god was Marduk. The people believed that Marduk had created the Earth.

The story begins when the ancient oceans, Apsu and Tiammat and their son Mummu, the mist, became angry with the younger gods, the Annunaki. Apsu and Mummu planned to kill the Annunaki, but their plot failed and Ea, god of earth and water, killed Apsu.

Tiammat wanted revenge for Apsu's death, so she created mad dogs, flying

Marduk with his bow and arrows.

dragons and other monsters to attack the Annunaki. Ea's son, Marduk the storm god, was persuaded to challenge Tiammat.

First Marduk had to arm himself for battle. He filled himself with fire and made seven hurricanes. Then he collected his weapons and rode into battle in his chariot of storms. Marduk killed Tiammat and divided her huge body to make the Earth and the sky. Then he created the stars and made men to put on the Earth.

The Hanging Gardens

The ruins of a huge vaulted structure stand to the north-east of the city, near the palace. This is believed to be the site of the magnificent Hanging Gardens, which the Greeks called one of the Seven Wonders of the World. The building measures 43 x 30 metres (140 x 100 ft). Writers who saw these wonderful gardens long after they were built describe a terraced structure, rising in smaller and smaller tiers, rather like the ziggurat or a green pyramid.

The outer walls were very thick; 7.5 metres (25 ft) is one estimate. The gardens were planted with palms, cypresses and other trees found in the Middle East, so each terrace must have held quite deep soil. Trailing plants tumbled over the edges of the walls, covering most of the brickwork.

The gardens were watered by a complicated system of pipes which brought water from the Euphrates. There are shafts under the main structure, which may have held pumps to raise the water. There may also have been waterfalls down the sides of the terraces.

Queen Amitiya would have welcomed the green shade of the gardens after the heat of the Babylonian sun. Filled with the scents of exotic flowers, they were a quiet haven in the bustling city.

The Walls of Babylon

As travellers approached Babylon, their first sight of the city would have been the massive walls that encircled it. First there was an enclosure surrounded by a high outer wall, where people from outside the city could shelter from invaders or other dangers. Then came the city walls themselves. The Greek historian Herodotus tells us that the city walls were so wide that two chariots, each one pulled by four horses, could drive along them side by side.

The city could be entered by nine gates in the walls. The most impressive of these was the Ishtar Gate. It was elaborately decorated with glazed tiles showing bulls, dragons and lions.

Beyond the Ishtar Gate, the sacred Processional Way led past the temple of Ninna and the royal palace to the religious centre of the city. Here stood the temple of Marduk and the great ziggurat or Tower of Babel itself. The royal palace was also the administrative centre of the empire, and many officials worked there.

Hills that were cities

Modern-day Iraq is dotted with thousands of mounds or 'tels'. Each one hides the remains of an ancient town or city. In 1899 the German archaeologist, Robert Koldewey, began to excavate the tel that hid Babylon. He spent the next 18 years uncovering the ancient city.

Koldewey had been an architect before becoming an archaeologist and this knowledge helped him to make the first accurate street plan of Babylon and work out what the mud-brick buildings must have looked like. But visitors to the city will not see many of the remains he uncovered. Most of his best finds are in museums in Berlin, Germany.

More recently, the Department of Antiquities of Iraq has continued Koldewey's work and has also rebuilt and restored some of the buildings. These include the Ishtar Gate and the temple of the goddess of birth, who was called Ninmar.

A section of the walls of Babylon.

Ishtar, the great goddess

If Marduk was the most important god in Babylon, Ishtar was the most important goddess because she ruled over two great essentials of life. She was the Lady of Sorrows and Battles as well as the radiant and beautiful goddess of love, known as the Lady of the Heavens.

Ishtar was not an easy goddess to please. She often took offence and would maliciously pursue anyone who annoyed her. She was well known for the number of husbands she had and how quickly they met an untimely death when she grew tired of them. Ishtar watched over the world as the planet Venus, so a star was one of her symbols. When she acted as the war goddess, her symbol was a lion.

Ishtar and her lion.

Hammurabi and his Law Code

King Hammurabi put together one of the clearest and most famous sets of laws of the ancient world. It was engraved on a huge slab of basalt for anyone to see and consult. At the top of the slab is a carving of Hammurabi with Sameth, the Babylonian god of justice. Underneath are the 282 laws. They include criminal laws and laws about owning slaves, debt, wages, marriage and divorce.

Punishments were very severe and worked on the principle of 'an eye for an eye and a tooth for a tooth'. The king probably did not make up all the laws himself – many of them may already have existed. What he did do was to set them out in permanent written form.

Hammurabi, from the Law Code stele.

Boghazköy

Turkey, c. 1700–1200 BC

From their fortified capital city high in the mountains of Anatolia, the powerful Hittite warriors waged war on the enemies who surrounded them.

On a high plateau in the centre of Anatolia in Turkey lived a warlike people called the Hittites. These are not the same Hittites that we read about in the Bible; they came from the area we know as Syria. The Anatolian Hittites were a short, sturdy race who became powerful between 1700 and 1200 BC. They had moved into Anatolia in about 2000 BC. The land they lived in was bleak and rocky, with cold, snowy winters, hot, dry summers, and heavy rains in spring. Why did they choose such a hostile landscape?

We know about the Hittites from records and other writings they left behind. They were as rugged as the craggy mountains they lived in.

The rocky mountains of Anatolia had one important advantage – they were easy to fortify against invaders. That is why the Hittites' capital city of Boghazköy was built on a mountain site.

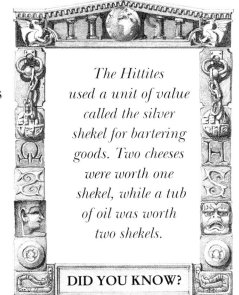

The Hittites used a unit of value called the silver shekel for bartering goods. Two cheeses were worth one shekel, while a tub of oil was worth two shekels.

DID YOU KNOW?

A mountain stronghold

Before about 1650 BC a city called Hattusas, or Hattusha, stood on the site that became Boghazköy. A Hittite leader called Labarnas realised that Hattusas was in a strong position, with sheer crags to the north and east. He rebuilt the fortress that stood there to give it solid walls and a palace. He made it his capital city and renamed himself King Hattusilis I. This was the start of the Hittite 'Old Kingdom' and a long line of kings who ruled from Boghazköy. Later kings extended the city and its fortifications until it became one of the most remarkable cities of ancient times.

The Hittite kings reigned over a large part of Anatolia, but their kingdom was completely surrounded by enemies who were constantly threatening to invade. The Hittites were always at war with one or other of their neighbours.

The Hittites' most effective weapons were chariots, which skilled charioteers drove at great speed. The warriors drove their chariots straight at lines of enemy foot soldiers, causing them to flee in terror.

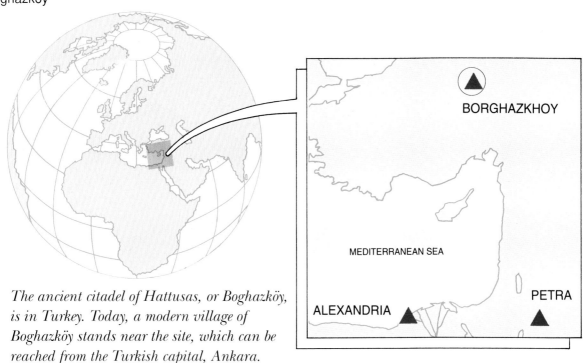

The ancient citadel of Hattusas, or Boghazköy, is in Turkey. Today, a modern village of Boghazköy stands near the site, which can be reached from the Turkish capital, Ankara.

We know about some of these enemies from Hittite documents, though we do not know where they all lived.

Mysterious kings

Boghazköy was heavily fortified against invasion. Walls divided the city into sections which could be defended more easily and the king's palace was surrounded by walls which cut it off from the rest of the city. This made the king seem remote from his people. They thought of him as a mysterious, god-like figure who had great power over them.

Around the palace were other buildings where the king's servants lived. We know that many people worked for him, including pages, doormen, grooms, a chamberlain, a doctor, a reciter of prayers and a personal bodyguard. All these people had to be

The king's gate in the city walls.

fed, so other buildings housed kitchens, pantries and a dairy.

A class-divided city

At the height of its power, a thriving community of about 30,000 people lived in the city outside the palace walls. They lived in houses of different shapes and sizes, depending on their social position in the the city. Slaves formed the lowest social class, followed by the farmers. The crops they cultivated included barley, emmer wheat, fruit, pulses, olives, onions and flax. They also tended cattle and sheep, and kept bees.

Next came the craftsmen, such as potters, carpenters, and cloth workers, who spun and wove the flax grown by the farmers. The cloth was used to make clothing. Hittite sculptures give us a good idea of what the people wore. Men wore knee-length tunics every day, with longer robes for important occasions. Women's clothes were similar, with long cloaks for the winter.

Top of the heap

Above the craftworkers in social ranking came the high officials and nobles. Nobles could be given land provided they swore to be loyal to the king and to provide extra troops in time of war.

When the Hittites conquered a neighbouring state, the king sent one of his nobles there as governor. The noble would gain wealth from the land, but in return he had to send the king tribute and military support. This meant that the king could draw on a well organised army of 30,000 soldiers when he needed to.

Crumbling power

We know from clay tablets found at Boghazköy that the Hittites had laws to help them rule their kingdom. But their main problem was fighting off invaders and keeping control in Anatolia. They gradually lost power as the Assyrians and other enemies began to take over important areas of land. In about 1200 BC the now much smaller Hittite kingdom was finally invaded by the Gasga people from the north. Boghazköy was burned to the ground some time in the 1180s BC.

Teshub, the weather god

The King of the Gods in the Hittite religion was Teshub, the weather god. According to legend, Teshub had taken over from his father, Kumarbi, as king of the gods and Kumarbi was angered by this. He created a huge stone monster, Ullikummi, to defeat the weather god. Teshub saw this huge figure rising up out of the sea and decided to fight it, but he was powerless against Ullikummi. The monster chased him out of his city.

Teshub asked for help from Ea, the god of wisdom. Ea ordered that the copper saw which had been used to divide heaven and earth should be brought to him, and with this he cut off the monster's head.

Teshub's queen was the goddess, Hebat, who is sometimes called the sun goddess of Arinna.

A carving of Teshub.

40

The citadel

You can still see the remains of the massive walls that enclosed the city. The walls sloped to stop enemies scaling them and attacking them with battering rams. Tunnels under the walls allowed the Hittites to creep out and attack their enemies from behind.

The streets of the city were straight and well planned. The houses were built of mud brick, with small windows and flat roofs made of dried mud and brushwood laid across wooden beams. Animals lived in the houses, which must have made life very smelly and cramped. The palace was like a small town itself. The royal family lived in apartments arranged around courtyards and there was a separate building for royal ceremonies.

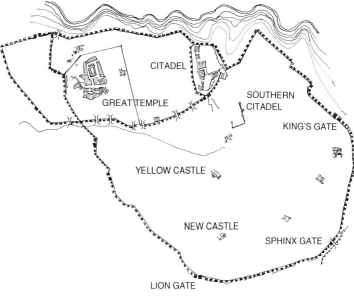

Carved gateways led into the city. At the top of the hill, behind more walls, were the palace buildings and the temple.

The Battle of Qadesh

The most famous Hittite victory was over the Egyptians at Qadesh. This battle was fought in about 1286 BC, near the end of the Hittites' reign of power. Boghazköy had already been ransacked by the Gasga people. The Hittite king, Mutwallis, had only just quelled that invasion when news arrived that the Egyptians were advancing towards the Hittite kingdom through northern Syria.

The king and his army met the Egyptians, under Rameses II, at the city of Qadesh in Syria. We know about the battle from Egyptian accounts, which admit that the Hittites were very skilful. They sent Rameses false information about the position of their troops and then won the battle by devising well-planned chariot attacks.

But there were more enemies waiting. The Assyrians and others were already sweeping in to take power. Even though the Hittites later formed an alliance with Egypt, when the daughter of King Hattusilis III married Rameses, it was too late to save the Hittite empire.

Egyptian painting of a battle scene.

The power behind the throne

Early Hittite kings were warrior leaders and their position was not very secure. There were often rebellions and murders as jealous nobles struggled for power. In 1500 BC, during the reign of King Telepinus, the rules for becoming king were fixed by law. From then on, the king had complete power over the people. He led the army, was chief judge and controlled every aspect of life.

The king and queen had to be present at big religious festivals and other important ceremonies. The queen was powerful in her own right. She played an important part in ceremonies and in the government of the country. If the king died first, the queen ruled the kingdom alone. Several queens seem to have had a great deal of influence. Queen Puduhepa, the wife of Hattusilis III, even wrote to the Queen of Egypt about state affairs.

Hittite queens identified with Hebat, the sun goddess.

Marvellous metalwork

The Hittites were skilled metalworkers and so they were keen to take control of lands where there were valuable supplies of metal ores. The first of the Old Kingdom rulers, King Hattusilis I, invaded Arzawa, in another part of Anatolia, which had valuable supplies of tin.

The Hittites also worked in copper and, much later in their history, their supplies were threatened when the Assyrians took control of an area around the upper Euphrates river. This contained the copper mines which provided the Hittites with most of their ore. As a result, the Hittite king, Tudhaliyas IV, invaded Cyprus which gave him another source of copper.

Iron was another important metal, particularly towards the end of the Hittite empire. In fact, the Hittites are supposed to be some of the earliest iron-workers in the world. Iron, which is strong but difficult to melt down and shape, was smelted (separated from the rock ore) near the iron mines in which it was found. It was then taken to forges at Boghazköy, where it was made into tools, weapons and probably armour. Several weapons have been found, including swords, daggers, axes and bows.

Hittite weapons.

A forgotten kingdom

Until about 150 years ago, no one had heard of the Hittites and their mountain kingdom. A French traveller and artist, Charles Texier, visited Turkey and discovered Boghazköy in 1834, but the kingdom of the Hittites remained a mystery until the beginning of this century. Then, in 1906, a German archaeologist Dr Hugo Winkler made an astounding discovery while excavating with a Turkish archaeologist called Dr Theodore Makridi. In the ruins of the citadel at Boghazköy, they unearthed thousands of clay tablets written in cuneiform script.

The tablets described the city which had once stood on the site and the people who lived there. There were tablets about their laws and their system of buying and selling goods. As the archaeologists worked, the history of this unknown people began to unfold. The story is still not complete. We are not sure where the Hittites came from or exactly how many kings they had, but new discoveries are still being made.

Today there is a small museum at the modern village of Boghazköy, which is about 128 kilometres (80 miles) east of the city of Ankara. The ruins of the citadel consist of walls and the foundations of buildings which show how it was built on its mountain crag. Other Hittite articles found on the site are now in museums in Ankara and Istanbul.

Karnak

Egypt, c. 1480–1080 BC

Massive temples and soaring columns make Karnak one of Egypt's most remarkable sights. But who worshipped in these temples? What do we know about the secret ceremonies carried out behind these ancient walls?

When people think of the ancient world, Egypt is one of the first places that springs to mind. It is full of amazing examples of a creative people who could fashion beautiful objects and build impressive temples and monuments. But even among such richness, Karnak stands out as one of ancient Egypt's most fascinating sights.

Karnak was built as a temple to the god Amun, but it much more than a temple. It is a whole religious complex, with great ceremonial halls and processional avenues watched over by sphinxes. This must have been one of the most important temple sites in ancient Egypt. Why was this?

The New Kingdom

The period of Egyptian history between 2050 and 1780 BC was known as the Middle Kingdom. The pharaoh ruled over the whole of Egypt, but local rulers who had been helpful to the royal family were allowed to govern their own provinces.

The Middle Kingdom ended when powerful rival groups began to fight each other. The most successful of these were the Hyksos, who had come from Palestine or Syria and settled around the Nile Delta. The Hyksos gradually took over more and more of Egypt.

The only kingdom to survive this unrest was Thebes in Upper Egypt. The Thebans drove out the Hyksos and in about 1550 BC the Theban prince, Ahmose, reunited Egypt and founded the New Kingdom.

The capital of the New Kingdom was at Thebes. The Theban kings began to build a new empire by pulling together the whole of Egypt and also taking over city-states in Syria, Lebanon, Israel and Jordan. As the empire grew, the pharaohs needed more and more officials to govern it.

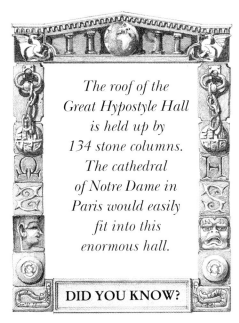

The roof of the Great Hypostyle Hall is held up by 134 stone columns. The cathedral of Notre Dame in Paris would easily fit into this enormous hall.

DID YOU KNOW?

The huge statues and giant columns covered with carved and painted decorations which surrounded the huge courtyards, towered above the priests and servants as they went about their daily business.

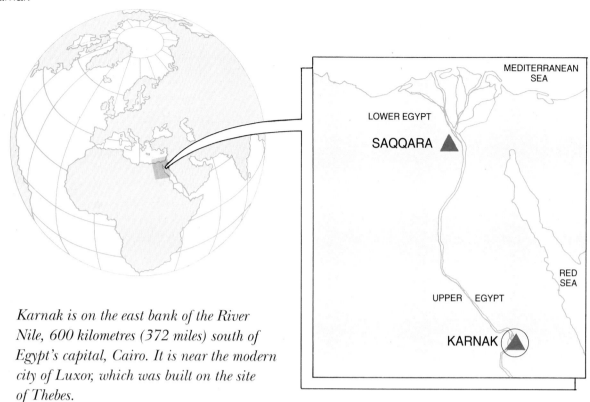

Karnak is on the east bank of the River Nile, 600 kilometres (372 miles) south of Egypt's capital, Cairo. It is near the modern city of Luxor, which was built on the site of Thebes.

They chose these administrators from the priests and scribes, so it is no surprise that there was a strong religious influence and that the complex of Karnak should have been built near Thebes.

A temple to Amun
Karnak was a holy site before the New Kingdom began. Archaeologists have discovered that temples existed there in the reign of King Senwosret I (1971–26 BC). But it was in the New Kingdom that it became the religious centre of Egypt.

The Egyptians worshipped hundreds of gods, but one of the most important was Amun, a sun god. The sun was a crucial part of life because it made the crops grow, and the Egyptians worshipped several different sun gods. But Amun was the most powerful; he had been given the title of King of the Gods during Senwosret's reign. Amun held his position as principal sun god for hundreds of years.

Hallowed hall
Karnak reached its peak during the reign of Rameses II (1290–24 BC), the pharaoh who fought the Hittites at Qadesh. Rameses was one of the longest-reigning kings of Egypt and he celebrated this fact with many elaborate building projects. He extended the temple of Amun at Karnak and completed the Great Hypostyle Hall – one of the largest single halls ever built.

Building work on the Great Hypostyle Hall began during the brief reign of Rameses I (1307–06 BC) and was continued by his son, Seti I (1306–1290), but still it was not finished. The work was eventually completed under Rameses II , so he took most of the credit for building the magnificent hall!

Holy, high and mighty
The priests were among the most powerful men in the land. On most occasions the temples were closed to

everyone except the king and the priests. It was believed that the priests had a special relationship with the gods, and as the pharaoh was a god-like figure himself, they had a special relationship with him as well.

The other thing that gave the priests power was the enormous following Amun had. He was worshipped all over Egypt and thousands of people worked in the temples as servants of the god. In fact, a papyrus document from the reign of Rameses III tells us that Amun had more than 80,000 servants and slaves. The temples also owned huge areas of land, as well as cattle and other animals which were sacred to Amun. The priests were in charge of all the temple property, which made them even more powerful.

A priest as pharaoh?

When the king and the priests were in agreement, the country ran smoothly, which strengthened Egypt's position in the world. But sometimes the priests tried to take over. In about 1080 BC, Hrihor, High Priest of Amun, claimed that he was king and tried to turn Egypt into a religious state. A wall carving at Karnak shows Hrihor making offerings to the gods. He is standing where the pharaoh would normally stand.

Hrihor's actions weakened Egypt's position. This, plus the fact that Egypt began to lose control of wealthy provinces such as Nubia, prompted several invasions. Egypt was taken over in turn by the Libyans, the Kushites and the Assyrians. From then on, Egypt was never truly independent again.

Local god makes good

Amun was originally a local god linked to a particular district – in his case, Thebes. He was already a national god by the time the New Kingdom began, but as Thebes grew into a powerful city, Amun became more and more important, until he was the principal god of Egypt.

He was represented in several forms as he gained importance. During the Middle Kingdom, he was the god of creation, and he was represented as a goose and then as a ram. Sometimes he was shown as a man with a ram's head.

At the height of his power Amun was a sun god and the god of the pharaohs. Some pictures show him as a man wearing a crown and carrying a sceptre and an ankh, the Egyptian symbol of life. In later pictures he is shown guarding over the pharaoh.

The Temple of Amun, Karnak

*The temple consists of a series of courtyards. Each of them is entered through a gateway known as a pylon. Flags probably flew in front of each pylon. In the courtyards were the ceremonial halls, called hypostyle halls because the roofs are held up with many columns (*stylos *is the Greek word for pillar).*

The temple complex was rebuilt and added to for hundreds of years. As you walk through the complex, you reach older and older parts. Today, visitors enter through the first pylon, which was built after the pharoahs.

In the time of Rameses II you would have entered through the second pylon. This leads to the Great Hypostyle Hall (top left) which covers an area of about 5000 square metres (54,000 sq. ft). In the back wall is the third pylon. This was the front entrance to the temple in the time of Amenhotep III (1391–53 BC).

Further back still there are three more pylons which lead to older parts of the temple. The oldest were built by Tuthmosis III (1479–25 BC).

The ruins at Karnak are massive, but archaeologists still have to reconstruct the whole picture. This picture shows what the temple probably looked like during the reign of Rameses II.

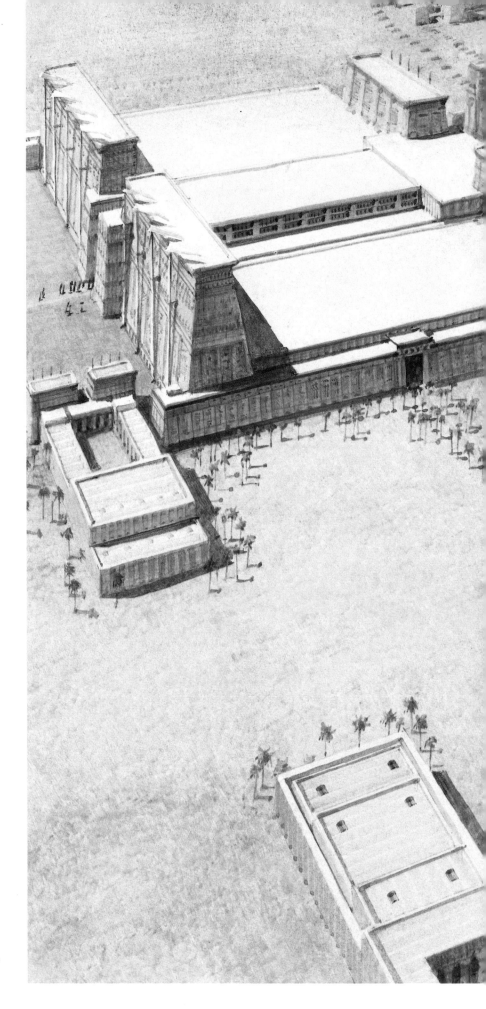

Worship ritual

Ordinary people did not often go to the great temples. They had little shrines in their homes dedicated to their household and local gods. Only the priests and the king were allowed into the temples.

The Egyptians believed that the gods would be sympathetic if they were given offerings every day. Temple carvings show us the basic ritual a priest went through. First he bathed in holy water, then he walked through the temple to the shrine. In this shrine was a statue of the god. The priest anointed the statue with oil and dressed it in fine clothes. Then a meal was spread out in front of the statue and the priest left the shrine. He walked backwards and swept the floor as he went to wipe away any footprints.

The priests were not worried by the fact that the gods never ate the food. This just showed that the gods were happy. The food was later taken away and given to the priests as payment for their duties.

A statue found at Karnak.

A god on earth

Throughout Egyptian history, the pharaoh was thought to be more than a man. He was a god who had taken on a man's form on earth. The people believed that he was responsible for keeping the whole universe in order, including the change of the seasons, the laws of nature and the movement of the stars in the sky. He was the only person who could reach the gods, so he must perform the proper ceremonies and make offerings so that the gods would look kindly on Egypt. When workers helped to build a temple or a pyramid for a pharaoh, they believed that they were helping to make Egypt more splendid in the eyes of the gods.

At Karnak, King Tuthmosis III had a statue of himself set up next to the statue of Amun in a part of the complex that was open to the public. People were encouraged to pray to the god-king as well as to the god himself. A wall painting see picture left shows King Amenophis III making an offering to his own god-like image.

Amenophis makes an offering to his statue.

Amun dethroned

There were some interruptions in Amun's reign as King of the Gods. The best known of these came during the reign of Akhenaten (1353–35 BC), who was originally called Amenhotep IV.

When Akhenaten came to the throne, he stated that all the Egyptian gods were false except one sun god. But it was not Amun-Ra. From now on, the only god to be worshipped was Aten, a sun god from earlier times. This decision caused a revolution. Akhenaten's officials closed down temples and threw out the priests. Monuments, statues and any other images of the gods, including Amun, were destroyed.

Aten was shown as a huge sun spreading rays which ended in human hands. The king created new rituals and ceremonies for his god and changed his own name from Amenhotep (meaning 'Amun is content') to Akhenaten ('it is well with Aten'). He even moved his capital city to Akhetaten ('horizon of Aten'), now called Tel el Amarna.

Most people were very unhappy with the new system of worship, but it did not last long. When Akhenaten died, his place was taken by Tutankhamun, the boy king, who brought back Amun and the other gods and began to rebuild the damaged temples and monuments.

Akhenaten makes an offering to Aten.

Restoring the ruins

Karnak is so enormous that it was never buried and hidden from view like many other sites. However, by the end of the last century large parts of it had collapsed. In 1895, the French archaeologist Georges Legrain began the huge task of clearing away the rubble, restoring columns to a standing position and rebuilding collapsed portions. During this work he discovered many sculptures, carvings and other items that had become buried under the sand and the fallen masonry.

Fellow French archaeologists Henri Chevrier and Pierre Lacau carried on with Legrain's work, and many other archaeologists have continued to work on this important site. Some details of Karnak's history cannot be filled in, even with the most painstaking work. For example, no one knows what the flags that flew in front of the pylons were like. After thousands of years, nothing remains of them.

Abu Simbel

Egypt, c. 1220 BC

*For over 3000 years, these giant statues of Rameses II have gazed
towards the rising sun. Behind them is a great temple cut deep into the cliff.
Why was it built here in Nubia?*

Near the banks of the River Nile in Upper Egypt stand four colossal statues of King Rameses II. They guard the entrance to the Great Temple at Abu Simbel. However, they are not in the centre of Egypt, near Thebes and other major cities. The temple was built on the southern edge of Rameses' kingdom, in an area called Nubia.

Nubia was a desert land which was no good for farming, but it was rich in precious metals, particularly gold. Throughout their history, the Egyptians fought for Nubia because they wanted control of these riches. But the Nubians were a warlike people and the battles were fierce. Egypt would gain control of Nubia after one battle, only to lose it again.

Under Egypt's control

Egyptian influence in Nubia was at its strongest during the reign of Rameses II. Control of Nubia had been in Egyptian hands since the reign of King Horemheb and had passed to Rameses I and then to Seti I, father of Rameses II. Each pharaoh had strengthened Egypt's hold over the Nubians but they were still rebellious. Rameses II was a famous soldier and he carried on the work of quelling outbreaks of fighting and improving Egypt's relations with Nubia.

Rameses was one of ancient Egypt's greatest builders, as sites such as Karnak show. He took gold from Nubia but he made some repayment by building a series of temples among the sandstone cliffs in Lower Nubia. The finest were two temples on the west bank of the Nile at Abu Simbel.

Power and glory

Why did Rameses choose to build such elaborate temples at Abu Simbel? Was it just to pay Nubia back for its gold? In fact, there could have been several other reasons as well. The four statues of

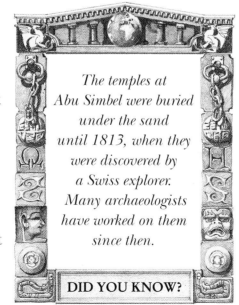

The temples at Abu Simbel were buried under the sand until 1813, when they were discovered by a Swiss explorer. Many archaeologists have worked on them since then.

DID YOU KNOW?

*The statues of Rameses, towering over passers-by, reminded the
Nubians who their ruler was. The Great Temple behind them is much more open than most
Egyptians temples, which were hidden away from the public.*

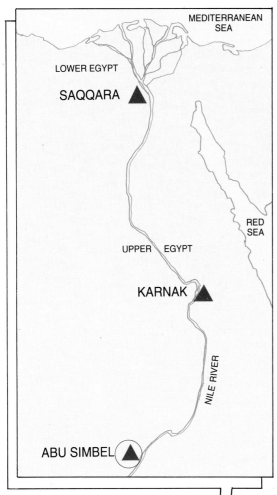

The temples at Abu Simbel stand by the Nile in Upper Egypt, 80 kilometres (50 miles) north of the second cataract of the Nile and 1230 kilometres (768 miles) south of Cairo.

Rameses outside the Great Temple are almost 20 metres (65 ft) tall. To the east stands a smaller temple, also guarded by massive statues of the king and his queen, Nofretari. With these colossal figures towering over them, how could the Nubians ever forget who their rulers were? And Abu Simbel was close to the edge of the Egyptian kingdom. A temple here showed that the king's power spread throughout the land.

Another more practical reason is that Abu Simbel had more fertile land than other parts of Nubia. Food could be grown there to support the army of workers needed to build the temples. In addition, Abu Simbel was probably a holy place before the Egyptians arrived, making it an obvious site for a temple. There was also a massive rock cliff for the stoneworkers to carve into.

Creating the temples

Until that time, most Egyptian temples and monuments had been built on flat ground. At Abu Simbel the architects decided to use a new method. The cliff itself became the temple. Workers tunnelled deep into the rock to create the temple chambers. The four statues of the king and the other statues and carvings on the outside were carved straight out of the rock face.

Rameses takes the credit for this scheme but, as with Karnak, he may have completed work begun by others. Inscriptions and carvings inside the temple show that it may have been planned and started during Seti's reign. Rameses would then have completed it and ordered the decoration and the carving on the outside.

Casting light on a dark secret

The statues of Rameses dominate the Great Temple and show his power as pharaoh. The statues are sitting on thrones carved with symbols of Upper and Lower Egypt. The pharaoh's relationship with the gods is also important. The temple is dedicated to three gods, Amun, Re-Harakhty and Ptah, and to Rameses, the god-king.

Amun's story is told in the chapter on Karnak. Re-Harakhty was another sun god, and Ptah was a god of creation and the god of craftsmen. Inscriptions on the statues link the king to the sun gods. 'The beloved one of the god Amun', one says. There are also statues of the three gods outside the Great Temple.

Inside the temple is a large hall with eight massive pillars. Each one shows Rameses wearing the double crown of Upper and Lower Egypt. There are more links between the king and the gods. One carving on the walls shows Rameses winning the Battle of Qadesh single-handed, helped by Amun. Legend says that Amun gave the king the strength of 10,000 men.

Behind the large hall is a smaller chamber and beyond that is the sanctuary, where offerings were made to the gods. The sanctuary was deep inside the cliff, so there were no windows. The walls were decorated with carvings and there were statues of the gods and the king, but the sanctuary was usually so dark that they were almost hidden from view. However, the temple was built in such a way that, at certain times of year, the light from the rising sun streamed in through the entrance and outer halls into the sanctuary. Suddenly the whole place was flooded with light.

A painting of Queen Nofretari.

Queen Nofretari

King Rameses II had a harem of wives, but Nofretari seems to have been his chief queen. Two enormous statues of her stand alongside four statues of Rameses outside the smaller temple at Abu Simbel.

Nofretari also had her own tomb in the Valley of the Queens at Thebes. It is one of the most beautifully decorated of all. Many of the paintings show Nofretari with a god or goddess. The inscription above one painting says, 'The Great Queen, the Mistress of Two Lands, Nofretari, beloved of the Goddess Mut, the justified, the one revered under the Great God, Osiris.' Another shows Nofretari being led through the underworld by the goddess Isis. Legends tell us that Osiris and Isis were the parents of Horus, the god of sun and sky.

The permanent power struggle

Egypt's relationship with Nubia was always unsettled. When the Egyptians had control, they were the conquerors or overlords of the Nubian people. Egyptian paintings show Nubians bringing tribute, including large rings of gold, to their masters.

Nubian prisoners of war.

Before Rameses' time, Nubian gold mines had never been worked properly because of a water shortage. An inscription at Kuban, near the mines, tells us that people who came to mine the gold died of thirst on the way. Seti I ordered his workers to dig wells but none of them produced water.

When Rameses was told of this problem, he commanded his workers to try his father's wells again. This time, they were to dig deeper. The plan worked. Water was found not far below the bottom of Seti's wells. Rameses could now take as much gold as he wanted, but in return he built the Nubian temples.

The actual work was carried out by Nubian slaves, who had been captured as prisoners of war during Egyptian battles with Nubia. We know about this from an inscription at Abu Simbel. Inscriptions in other parts of the Egyptian empire show that it was usual for the pharaohs to use prisoners of war in this way.

The god Horus

The symbol of the Egyptian sun god, Re-Harakhty, was the rising and setting sun. His name is a combination of two other sun gods, Re and Horus. Re or Ra was the principal sun god of Egypt before Amun. Horus was the god of the sky, as well as of the sun and is usually shown with a hawk's head. Re-Harakhty actually means 'Horus of the horizon', giving the idea of the sun rising in the east.

Horus was worshipped throughout Egypt and he was given different names and images in different areas. He was the son of Osiris and Isis. Ancient stories say that Osiris was murdered by his brother Set. Horus was brought up secretly in the swamps around the delta until he was old enough to fight Set. Many long and fierce battles followed but nobody won. In the end, there was a formal trial and a judgement was made against Set.

Horus, the hawk-headed sun god.

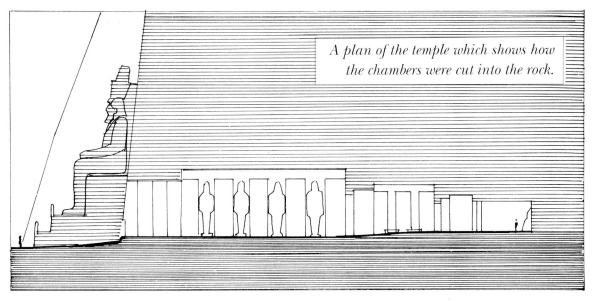

A plan of the temple which shows how the chambers were cut into the rock.

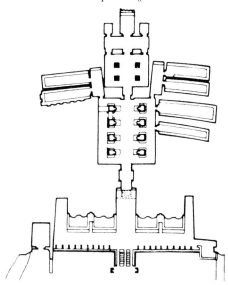

Ground plan of the Grand Temple.

The moving temples

The temples at Abu Simbel found new fame in the 1960s. The annual flooding of the Nile had always caused problems, so it was decided to build a dam at Aswan to control it. The planners realised that this would raise the level of the river, flooding many of the Nubian temples. Several different schemes were suggested to save the temples, particularly those at Abu Simbel.

One suggestion was to raise the temples on hydraulic jacks. Another was to build a massive concrete raft under the temples so that they would float as the water level rose. In the end, the suggestion that was agreed upon was to move the temples, stone by stone, to a higher site.

The stone had to be cut up before it could be moved and this was a delicate operation. Large mechanical saws were used to cut up the blocks underneath but the surface carvings were cut with specially designed saws so that no details would be lost. The next problem was lifting the stones.

Sandstone is a soft rock and lifting equipment would ruin the carvings, so steel bolts were driven into hidden areas of the stone and then attached to cranes for lifting.

The Great Temple and the smaller temple were rebuilt higher up the same cliff. They were positioned in the same way, so the rising sun streamed through the entrance. This fantastic feat is the latest chapter in the incredible history of Abu Simbel.

Khorsabad

Iraq, 720–705 BC

*The Assyrians had a reputation for great cruelty, yet their king, Sargon II,
built a magnificent city at Khorsabad. Were the Assyrians
really what they seemed, and why was Sargon's city deserted after his death?*

In northern Mesopotamia, among the rolling hills between the upper Tigris and Euphrates rivers, lived the Assyrians, a people who were to become the most feared in the ancient world. But were these people simply cruel barbarians? Their art and the great cities they left behind tell us that they were not. Of these cities, Khorsabad is the most mysterious. It was built by King Sargon II, but left deserted at the end of his reign. What is the history behind this strange city?

The birth of an empire

The Assyrians had broken away from the Sumerian civilisation after the fall of Ur in about 2000 BC. Like most of the people in the Mesopotamian valley, they were farmers who made use of the fertile soil for growing barley and for raising cattle, sheep and goats. Their base was the city-state of Assur, in what is now northern Iraq. From here they built other city-states, such as Nineveh and Arbela.

The Assyrians began to build up their empire in about 1363 BC but there were constant wars between them and their neighbours in the struggle for power. The most successful king during this period was Tiglath-pileser (1114–1076 BC), who was a strong military leader and developed the skilful use of chariots and well-designed iron weapons for warfare. By about 1100 BC, the Assyrians controlled an empire which stretched from the Mediterranean north to what is now eastern Turkey.

There was a period of decline after Tiglath-pileser's reign, but eventually another strong king, Tiglath-pileser III (744–27 BC) came to the throne. He took control of Syria and Babylon, and set up a system of taxation and

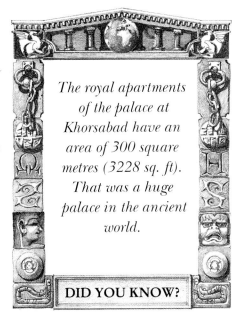

The royal apartments of the palace at Khorsabad have an area of 300 square metres (3228 sq. ft). That was a huge palace in the ancient world.

DID YOU KNOW?

*The Assyrians took advice from soothsayers about important events.
Here, a soothsayer points the way to the new city. Sargon may have taken advice when choosing
his site for Khorsabad. In the background is an example of a carved relief.*

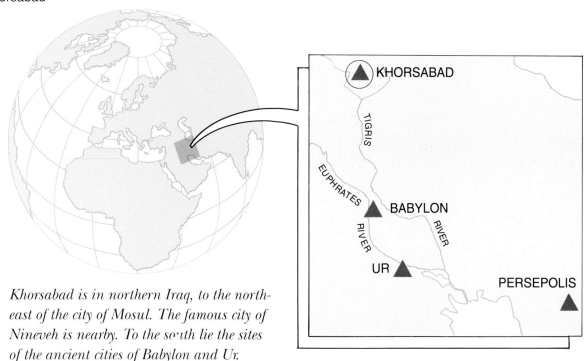

Khorsabad is in northern Iraq, to the northeast of the city of Mosul. The famous city of Nineveh is nearby. To the south lie the sites of the ancient cities of Babylon and Ur.

military control. When Sargon II came to the throne in 721 BC, he took over a large, well-organised empire.

King Sargon

Sargon was probably not a descendant of the Assyrian kings but he took the name of an early king, Sargon of Akkad, the world's first empire builder. The first Sargon was an almost legendary figure, so adopting his name gave the new king power from the first. But he soon proved himself a successful ruler in his own right. Syria and Babylonia fought to break free from Assyrian control but Sargon quelled them.

But he was not just a military leader. Documents have been found which say that he rebuilt villages which had fallen into disrepair, opened canals, and founded a library to encourage scholars. He also encouraged artists and craftsmen. His palaces were decorated with exquisite wall reliefs, and Assyrian craftsmen excelled in making glass and metal-working.

The non-stop builder

Sargon's reign was successful but the king was restless. He could not settle in one city. He began in Assur, where he repaired the walls and decorated the temple. Then he moved to Kalhu and rebuilt the royal palace. His next stop was Nineveh, where again he restored the temple.

Sargon may have behaved in this way to show these cities what wonderful buildings he could give them and make them loyal to him. But all the cities had fine buildings before Sargon came on the scene. None of them was a city that he had created. There was only one way to have a city that was all his own, and that was to build one from scratch. And so he ordered work to begin on the city that the Assyrians called Dur Sharrukin, the City of Sargon. Today we know it as Khorsabad.

A dream city

Sargon and his architect, Tab-shar Ashur, planned the city carefully. The site was on clay soil, which was good for brick-making. The city itself was large and more or less square, with four walls around it.

Inside the walls was a maze of narrow streets. The houses were probably single-storey, mud-brick buildings with a courtyard in the centre. The windows would have faced on to the courtyard, not on to the street.

Near the north wall of the city stood Sargon's royal palace. The carved reliefs from the walls show us fascinating details of the Assyrian empire. Some of the carvings show the violence the Assyrians used in battle. The Bible tells us of their cruelty and the poet Byron describes their invasion of Jerusalem in 701 BC, 'The Assyrian came down like the wolf on the fold'.

But in fact the Assyrians were not as bloodthirsty as they seemed. They used terror tactics in battle, but they were not cruel to nations they had conquered. So long as people paid their taxes, they left them alone.

Assyrian bureaucracy

The empire was divided into provinces, with Assyrian governors who reported to the king. Each governor had officials and soldiers to keep law and order. About 2000 letters between the capital and the provinces have been found, which shows that communications were good.

So what happened to Khorsabad? In 705, Sargon was killed in battle. The Assyrians, took this as a bad omen, so Sargon's son and heir, Sennacherib, left Khorsabad and made Nineveh his capital city. The Assyrians never returned to Sargon's city.

Sargon of Akkad

Sargon II took his name from Sargon of Akkad, who ruled over northern Mesopotamia, then known as Akkad, and conquered the Sumerians in about 2300 BC. No one is sure why Sargon of Akkad became king, except that he was a strong leader. Perhaps that is why Sargon II took his name.

Sargon of Akkad is surrounded by mystery and legend. Assyrian documents tell us that he claimed he was made king by the gods. He said that he was the son of a holy woman at the temple. She was not allowed to have children, so when her baby was born, she put him into a basket and cast him on to the river. The river carried him downstream until he was found by Akki, who was drawing water. Akki brought Sargon up as his son and later made him a gardener in the temple. Sargon claimed that while he was at the temple, the goddess Ishtar helped him to rise to power.

A bronze head of Sargon of Akkad.

The royal palace at Khorsabad

We know about the palace from the ruins and wall reliefs which have been found, and also from letters between Sargon and the architect. The palace was huge. There was a large domestic area containing kitchens, a bakery, store rooms and stables. The main entrance led into a vast courtyard. On the left of the courtyard was the temple area, which contained several small temples and a seven-stepped ziggurat. On the

right were some domestic buildings. The royal apartments were straight ahead. Beyond these were the state chambers, including the throne room which was 46 metres (150 ft) long.

Visitors approached the throne room through another huge courtyard. As they entered they saw long walls covered with carved reliefs of winged, human-headed bulls leading to the king on his throne. These mythical creatures are thought to

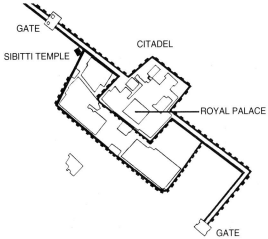

GATE

SIBITTI TEMPLE

CITADEL

ROYAL PALACE

GATE

show Gilgamesh, the legendary Mesopotamian hero. They guarded the throne and illustrated the power of the king.

The palace was decorated with flamboyant carvings of the Assyrians conquering their empire. There are battle scenes, with charging chariots, fighting soldiers and fleeing enemies. Other carvings show the Assyrians hunting elephants and lions.

63

Gilgamesh the hero

Gilgamesh, the legendary king of the Sumerian city-state of Uruk, is one of the earliest known heroes. His adventures are described in a poem, the *Epic of Gilgamesh*, which was found on twelve clay tablets written in Akkadian script in an ancient library in Nineveh.

Gilgamesh really did exist. There are records about a war between him and the king of Kish, but because early kings were linked with the gods, they are steeped in legend and it is difficult to separate fantasy from reality.

In the poem, Gilgamesh is shown as a heroic figure, 'two-thirds god and one-third man'. He and his companion Enkidu, a man from the wilderness who was brought up by the wild animals, have many adventures. Then Enkidu becomes ill and dies, and Gilgamesh is so distressed that he sets out to find the secret of eternal life. His journey takes him through many dangers to the Ocean of Death, where he asks the ferry-man, Urshanabi, to take him across.

On the other side he meets Utnapishtim, an immortal semi-god. Gilgamesh asks him how he became immortal. Utnapishtim tells him that the gods were annoyed by noisy people who kept them awake, so they planned to send a great flood which would destroy mankind. However, one of the gods, Ea the wise, told Utnapishtim about the flood, so he built a boat and took his family and many animals on board. At first Enlil, the storm god, was angry that Utnapishtim survived the flood, but Ea persuaded him to grant Utnapishtim and his wife immortality.

Utnapishtim then tells Gilgamesh about a plant which grows on the sea bed. He says that it will at least make old people young again. Gilgamesh ties stones to his feet, dives down and picks the plant.

On his journey back to Uruk he stops to bathe at a well, where a serpent steals the plant, sheds its skin and disappears. The story ends here, with Gilgamesh realising that people must grow old and die.

Winged beasts, from the palace walls.

A lost city of Mesopotamia

Khorsabad was first excavated by the French archaeologist Paul Emile Botta in the middle of the nineteenth century. It was buried under a mound known as a 'tel'. Victor Place took over his work in 1851. Place made the first plans of the city and worked out what the buildings would have looked like.

Between 1928 and 1935, more work was done by the Oriental Institute of the University of Chicago in America. They revised some of Place's plans and also uncovered more areas of the city, including temples and public buildings. The tablets containing the *Epic of Gilgamesh* were found by archaeologists excavating the library of Assurbanipal, the last king of the Assyrian empire.

The mud-brick houses of the ordinary people of Khorsabad have long since disappeared, but archaeologists have found stones which show that the streets were paved. It is easier to see what the palace was like because the foundations are still there.

Army of fear

The Assyrians could not have been so powerful without an efficiently organised army. They used foot soldiers, cavalry and charioteers. Sargon improved the tactics of the foot soldiers and made good use of bowmen. He also introduced larger chariots which could hold a driver, a bowman and one or two shield bearers. The army used battering rams to invade and besiege cities.

Sargon kept his army trained and ready at all times. He led the army himself but he had a well-organised team of commanders under him. Wall reliefs show the army on the march. First came the standard bearers, followed by the king and his bodyguards. Behind them was a cavalry unit, with foot soldiers on either side, ready to go into battle immediately. Then came the main army, followed by wagons carrying food and equipment such as battering rams.

Assyrian soldiers, from a wall relief.

Persepolis

Iran, c. 520–330 BC

The magnificent palace of Persepolis was the meeting point of the ancient world under the Persian emperors. But why was it built in such a lonely place? What ceremonies took place in its sumptuous rooms?

In the sixth century BC a new and powerful force swept over the Middle East like a tidal wave and created the largest empire the world had ever seen. The Persians, based in what is now Iran, took only a few years to conquer territories as far apart as Egypt, Babylon and India. At the same time, they took home ideas from the conquered lands and so created a unique new culture in their own land.

A land of great palaces, Persia has always been associated with the rich and exotic. Merchants from the East carried silk, spices and gold through Persia to the western lands. The Three Wise Men who brought gifts to the infant Christ were probably priests or magi of the Persian religion, Zoroastrianism. Persian kings built great, ornate palaces throughout their kingdom as a symbol of their power.

The vast palace at

Persepolis was built by Darius, the king who ruled the empire at the height of its power. Its architecture is a mixture of Greek, Egyptian, Assyrian and Persian, blended together in a unique design. But the puzzling thing about Persepolis is that it was built in the middle of nowhere – 480 kilometres (300 miles) away from the capital city of Susa. So who were these people who suddenly rose up to create a mighty empire, and what is the secret of the lonely palace at Persepolis?

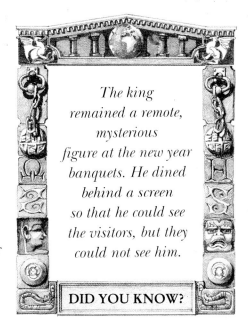

The king remained a remote, mysterious figure at the new year banquets. He dined behind a screen so that he could see the visitors, but they could not see him.

DID YOU KNOW?

The earliest kings

The first kings of Persia were from Media, the mountainous region of western Iran. The Medes were tough people, used to fighting off warlike neighbours such as the Assyrians. The earliest king of Media was called Haxamanish or Achaemenes, so the people were known as the Achaemenids. When they expanded their

A noble sits under one of the brooding sculptures of the Persian kings which decorated the columns and doorways of Persepolis. The all-powerful king seemed to watch over his subjects everywhere they went.

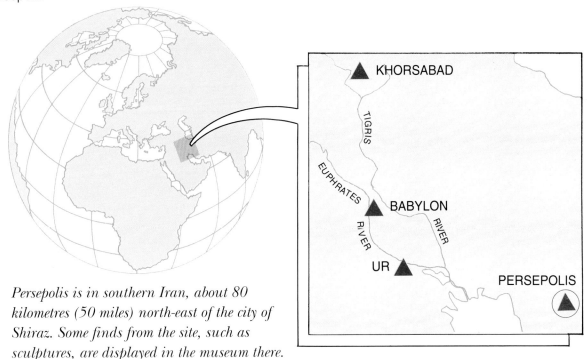

Persepolis is in southern Iran, about 80 kilometres (50 miles) north-east of the city of Shiraz. Some finds from the site, such as sculptures, are displayed in the museum there.

territory into Persia, the Persians also became known as Achaemenids.

The first powerful Median king was Cyaxeres. In 614 BC, he made an alliance with Babylon by marrying his daughter, Amitiya, to Nebuchadnezzar. Then, in 612 BC, he conquered the Assyrian capital of Nineveh. This was a tremendous victory for Cyaxeres. Nineveh was ruined and the empire of the Persians began to expand.

Tentacles of power

The next king was Cyrus the Great (559–29 BC). He was known as the emperor of the Medes and the Persians. Cyrus was the king who conquered Babylon in 539 BC, but he treated the Babylonians well and they came to look upon him as their rightful leader. He also released the Jews who had been imprisoned in Babylon and allowed them to go home to Palestine, so he gained a stronghold there as well.

Cyrus did not try to take over the peoples he conquered. He adopted the best aspects of their laws and religion for the empire, but he left them free to carry on their lives as before.

Cyrus's son, Cambyses, succeeded him and ruled in a similar way. His main achievement was to conquer Egypt in 525 BC. Libya also surrendered to the Persians. Cambyses stayed in Egypt for three years. He was called back to Persia in 522 but died on the way home, and his cousin, Darius, became king.

Darius took over an already large empire and expanded it by adding parts of northern India. He also improved the way in which the empire was organised, began a massive road-building scheme, and built Persepolis.

The lonely place Darius chose to build his new palace was near the southern mountains, well away from the bustle of his capital city Susa. The climate was cool and pleasant and Darius could escape from the centre of his now vast empire. Shutting himself away in a palace miles from anywhere set the king apart from the people and gave him an air of mystery.

Work on the palace began in 520 BC and it took at least sixty years to complete, through the reign of Darius and the next two kings, Xerxes and Artaxerxes. Craftsmen came from all over the empire to help with the building work. That is why it is built in a range of styles.

However, the palace is not just a hotchpotch of styles copied from elsewhere. The Persian kings wanted their palace to be different from anywhere else, so the various styles were adapted to suit the overall design.

The king did not live at Persepolis all the time, but the palace was more than a country retreat. Every March, officials from every corner of the empire crowded into the small town near the palace to celebrate the new year. They brought the king and his family gifts of jewellery, clothing and even animals such as horses, giraffes and camels.

They approached the palace in a long, colourful procession led by marching soldiers, chariots and horsemen. The king waited in the audience hall to receive them. Afterwards, everyone was entertained at an enormous banquet.

Roads to success

Darius divided his great empire into provinces and appointed governors and officials to run them. But the king did not want these officials to have too much power. He wanted to keep firm control of the empire. Travel had to be made as quick and easy as possible, so Darius built a road right across his empire from Susa, which was just north of the Persian Gulf, to Sardis near the Aegean Sea. The road was 2683 kilometres (1677 miles) long and linked Lydia, Phrygia, Babylonia and Assyria with Susa.

Royal messengers could now ride between Susa and any of the provinces fairly easily. There were 111 post stations along the road where horses could be changed. Inns were set up to provide food for travellers.

Building a road like this was an incredible feat in the ancient world. It opened up many more possibilities for the whole empire. People from all over the empire were brought together and trading was easier. It made huge gatherings, like the new year ceremonies at Persepolis, possible. Artists and craftsmen from all over the empire could bring their skills to the royal palaces of Persia. And it was easier for Darius and his successors, Xerxes and Artaxerxes, to keep in touch with the people.

King Artaxerxes on his throne.

The palace complex

Today, only the foundations of many of the palace buildings are still there. We can see from these that most of the rooms contained many columns to hold the roof up.

In the throne room and audience hall, or apadana, the columns were 20 metres (65 ft) tall. They were decorated with carvings, and the tops, or capitals, were often carved with the heads of animals, such as bulls and roaring lions. The rooms were lavishly decorated with coloured tiles, gold ornaments and hangings of gold lace.

The most important building apart from the audience halls was the royal treasury. The kings kept all their riches here, away from the crowds in the city. There were precious metals and jewels, weapons and carpets. Much of the kings' wealth came from tribute brought to the new year celebrations at Persepolis.

1. STAIRWAY TO TERRACE

2. GATEWAY OF XERXES

3. INNER GATEHOUSE

4. HALL OF 1000 COLUMNS

5. AUDIENCE HALL

6. TRIPYLON

7. HAREM

8. TREASURY

9. PALACES

The Persians and the Greeks

Darius was the first Persian ruler to describe himself as the 'King of Kings'. Throughout his empire, people thought of him as master of the world. But just then another powerful people, the Greeks, were preparing to challenge his supremacy.

At the beginning of Darius's reign, Greece was part of his empire, but in about 499 BC the Ionian city-states on the Asian mainland rebelled against Persian rule. Athens sent twenty ships of soldiers to help them, but the Persians managed to crush the rebellion. This was just the start of the revolution, however. The cities of

Eretria, Athens and Sparta stood up to Darius, and in 490 BC he sent an army to quell the upstart Greeks.

The Battle of Marathon

At first it seemed that the Greeks could not win. Eretria fell to the Persians and the army prepared to march to Athens. But the Athenians used surprise tactics. Instead of waiting for the invasion, they marched on the Persians instead, forcing them back into their ships which lay in the Bay of Marathon. The Persians had to retreat.

The Battle of Marathon, as this incident was called, was the Persians' first defeat. Four years later, Darius died and his son, Xerxes, came to the throne. Although Darius had ruled over a stable empire for more than thirty years, there had been problems under the surface. The king had taxed his people very heavily, and they were discontented. When he died, the unrest erupted in rebellions in Egypt and Babylonia. But the main problem was still the Greeks.

Victory over the Persians

In 480 BC Xerxes led a huge army against Athens and Sparta. The Persians defeated the Athenian and Spartan armies at Thermopylae, north of Athens. Then they marched on to the city itself.

But this time the Greeks were ready for them. The Athenian general, Themistocles, had persuaded the Greeks that they could defeat the Persians most easily at sea. They agreed to build a fleet of 200 sailing ships called triremes, which were lighter and faster than the Persian ships.

As the Persians advanced,

A Libyan tribute-bearer.

Dignitaries visit Persepolis.

The Athenians suggested uniting the city-states into an organisation called the Delian League. Each city gave ships, or money to build them. The ships were added to the Athenian navy, which brought more wealth and power to Athens. The Delian League gradually became the Athenian empire.

Xerxes and the Persians fought on, but they finally lost all their power in Europe. However, they still held most of the Middle East when Xerxes died in 465 BC. He was succeeded by his son, Artaxerxes, who ruled for forty years. He finished the throne room, the 'hall of a hundred columns', at Persepolis and continued to hold court there. By now, rebellions were breaking out all over the empire. A long period of unrest followed and many Persian kings met violent deaths as they tried to hold on to the empire.

Themistocles ordered everyone to leave Athens. The women and children were taken to safety, and the men boarded the Greek triremes to fight at sea.

The Greeks lured the Persian ships into position by sending Xerxes a false message. The message said that the Greek fleet was trying to escape, so Xerxes sent his warships to block their route. The Greek ships were waiting to attack them, and the Persians lost most of their ships in the battle. Their army was finally destroyed by the Spartans in a land battle at Plataea in 479 BC.

Then, in 334 BC, Alexander the Great led a Greek army of 40,000 men across the Dardanelles and conquered the Persian army at Issus, on the Mediterranean coast. He pushed on to conquer Babylon and Susa. In 330 BC the last Persian king, Darius III, was murdered and Persepolis was destroyed.

Greece triumphant

The Greeks were becoming more and more powerful. The Athenians had the best navy and they made it even larger after the victory at Salamis. The Spartans had a strong army because all Spartan men became soldiers when they left school and spent their lives training and preparing for war. But the Greeks were still worried about invasions from the Persians.

A carving from the palace.

Zoroaster the prophet

Despite its odd name, the Persian religion, Zoroastrianism, does not seem too strange to us because it has similarities with Christianity. But when it began to take a hold in Persia in the reign of Cyrus the Great, it was revolutionary.

The early Persians had worshipped several different gods, who had to be kept happy with animal sacrifices offered to them by the magi. The religion of Zoroastrianism centred round only one god, called Ahuramazda (meaning 'wise lord'). Zoroaster was a prophet who founded the religion after he had a vision in which Ahuramazda told him of his quest for good in the world, and his constant struggles against the evil spirit, Ahriman. If people behaved well, the god told Zoroaster, they would help Ahuramazda to win the fight against Ahriman and so have everlasting life.

But who was Zoroaster? To worshippers of the new religion, he was not an ordinary man. His mother, a girl of fifteen, was visited by a divine being which filled her with glory. Her father, who was influenced by the evil spirits, thought she was bewitched and sent her away from home. She then married and Zoroaster's spirit was sent to her by the angels in the juice of the haoma plant, which was drunk by the magi as part of their religious ceremonies.

When Zoroaster was born, everyone rejoiced, but the evil spirits tried to destroy him throughout his childhood. When he was thirty years old, Zoroaster had his first vision and began to preach about the new faith. He did not have much success until he travelled to eastern Iran and managed to convert the local king, Vishtaspa. When Cyrus brought Vishtaspa's region under the control of the Persian empire, Zoroastrianism began to spread and Zoroaster himself went to the king's court where he had more influence still.

The god Ahuramazda.

How Alexander destroyed Persepolis

From the time of Darius until the end of the Persian Empire, Persepolis had been the meeting point of the ancient world. The annual visit of dignitaries from all over the empire, the riches stored in its treasury, and its magnificence had made it a true symbol of the Persian kings' power.

But when Alexander the Great brought the whole empire under Greek control, he had no use for the great, remote palace so far from home. After the murder of Darius III by one of his own generals, no more processions came to Persepolis to pay tribute, so Alexander had the palace burned to the ground. The stones that remained were lost under the sand until the 1920s, when archaeologists began work there. As well as the foundations of the palace, they discovered carvings, including scenes of the processions bringing gifts to the king.

Burning down Persepolis was strange behaviour for Alexander. Perhaps he wanted revenge for the many years of warfare. But in other ways he tried to adapt to the Persian way of life. He suggested that his men should marry Persian women and, to set an example, he himself married a Persian woman, Roxane from Sogdiana.

A cuneiform record tablet.

Ruling the empire

The Persian empire was divided into provinces called satrapies. Each one was under the command of a governor or satrap, who was directly responsible to the king. This system worked well when there was a strong king on the throne, but if the king was weak, the satraps could become too powerful and start ruling their provinces like kings in their own right.

Darius realised this when he came to the throne, so he made sure that all the satraps were Persian rather than people from the conquered lands. He did not give them absolute power over their provinces, and each satrap had an army commander who reported directly to the king.

Tax collectors also reported straight to the king, which gave Darius control over the finances of the empire. Each province had secretaries who were known as the 'king's eyes and ears'; many of them were Darius's relatives. They kept the king informed about the way the provinces were being governed.

Petra

Jordan, c. 170 BC – AD 100

*For centuries the city of Petra lay hidden among the desert hills.
No one in the Western world knew it existed. So who built this strange city and
why was it forgotten for so long?*

Of all the mysteries of the ancient world, the lost city of Petra, hidden away in the Jordanian desert, must be one of the most incredible. Petra is so well concealed among the hills that it lay undiscovered by the Western world until 1812. The architecture of the city is a classical mixture of Persian, Assyrian, Greek and Roman styles. Yet the people who carved this 'rose-red city' out of the sheer desert crags are almost unknown today.

So who were they? How did they have the knowledge to carve these ornate classical buildings? And if they were so skilled, why are they not famous today, like the Egyptians, Greeks and Romans? Most extraordinary of all, why did they choose to build their city in a place that was so difficult to get to?

Settling down

Petra was built by a tribe called the Nabataeans, who were nomads from the northern Arabian desert. They seem to have moved northwards from there to an area known as Edom, now in southern Jordan, around the 530s and 520s BC, and to have mixed peacefully with the Edomites who lived there.

By about 350 BC, the Nabataeans had given up their nomadic lifestyle. They settled in Edom and started to build Petra. They supported themselves by keeping animals and by trading with the Arabian peoples. But why did they decide to settle? And why in Petra?

Caravans in the desert

The Nabataeans realised that the site of Petra was near some of the ancient world's most important trade routes. One major route was along the valley which links the Dead Sea with the Gulf of Aqaba in the Red Sea. Caravans of merchants travelled along the eastern coast of the

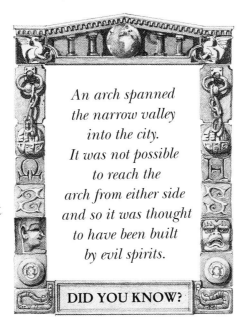

*An arch spanned the narrow valley into the city.
It was not possible to reach the arch from either side and so it was thought to have been built by evil spirits.*

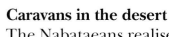

DID YOU KNOW?

*The Khasneh (treasury) was built with two rows of columns, in classical Greek style.
In front there are bustling streets and market stalls. Travellers
from all over Asia met here to exchange goods on their way along the trade routes.*

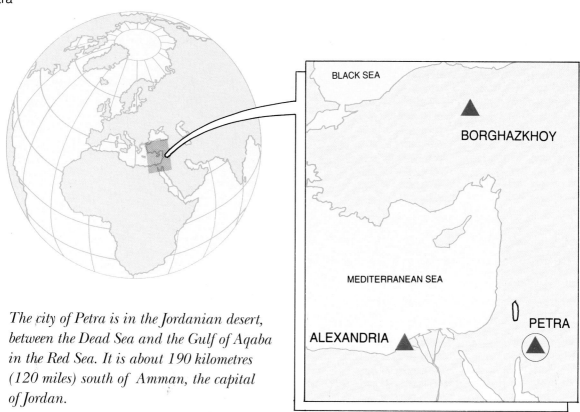

The city of Petra is in the Jordanian desert, between the Dead Sea and the Gulf of Aqaba in the Red Sea. It is about 190 kilometres (120 miles) south of Amman, the capital of Jordan.

Dead Sea from Damascus to Aqaba and on into Arabia. The caravan sometimes needed to stop for supplies of fresh water, and Petra, halfway along the route, made an ideal stopping-off place.

An east-west route connecting Mesopotamia with Egypt also passed Petra. This later became part of the famous silk road that stretched from China to the Mediterranean, where ships waited to take silks and spices from the east to Greece and Rome. A third route went by Petra to the Mediterranean port of Gaza.

The Nabataeans saw that they could become rich and powerful by controlling the trade that passed through the crossroads at Petra. At first they were probably no better than bandits, lying in wait for the caravans. They would take what they wanted but leave the merchants enough to make it worth their while using the route.

A more organised system was to tax the caravans as they passed through. The people of Petra also controlled the caravans by offering themselves as paid guides through the difficult rocky terrain of their land.

There is very little written evidence about how the Nabataeans lived at this time, but they seem to have extended the territories they controlled. Nabataean kings are mentioned in the 160s BC and we know that they rose to such power that they ruled towns as far apart as Damascus and Gaza.

Treasury or tomb?

Visitors to Petra take the only way into the city, through a narrow rocky gorge known as the Siq. For about half an hour they travel on foot or on horseback through this silent valley, with nothing to be seen but sheer cliffs towering about 25 metres (80 ft) above them. It is dark and gloomy. Then suddenly, as they round the last bend, they are facing one of Petra's most remarkable buildings – the Khasneh.

It is a sight to make even the most experienced traveller gasp. The front of the building, cut straight into the rock face, is about 30 metres (100 ft) wide and 40 metres (130 ft) tall. It is decorated with two rows of pillars topped by carved pediments. In the centre, at the very top, is a large urn.

There are different stories about the Khasneh. Its elegant Greek-style columns suggest that it was built by workers from outside the area. But who and why? We do not know. Another mystery is how the Khasneh was used. The word 'khasneh' means 'treasury' and the Bedouin people who lived around the city thought that the urn contained hidden stores of gold. They peppered it with bullets from their rifles to try to release the treasure.

Another possibility is that the Khasneh was a tomb, perhaps to King Aretas III (86–62 BC), who extended the Nabataean lands to Damascus and Syria. Aretas was known to have been interested in Greek architecture.

The city of tombs

An eerie thing about Petra is that it is full of tombs – about 4000 of them. It is hard to believe that living people ever walked its streets. The tombs are all cut out of the rocks in the hillsides around the city, so they have survived the desert wind and rain. The large open space in the floor of the valley would have contained many mud-brick houses, shops and other buildings which have long since collapsed in ruins.

The designs of the tombs range from simple holes in the rock, with hardly any decoration, to magnificent classical designs – but who was buried in them? Once again, we do not know. We know that they worshipped their kings and made them into gods when they died. Perhaps the more splendid buildings are the tombs of the Nabataean kings.

Left to right: Ionic, Doric, Corinthian.

Greek column designs

The columns on the Khasneh are in the Corinthian style. This is the most ornate of the three Greek styles of architecture. The oldest and simplest style was the Doric, which was used in ancient Greece from about 700 BC. The Parthenon in Athens has Doric columns. They are thicker than later styles and very strong, with a plain stone slab at the top.

The Ionic style dates from about 500 BC. The columns are slimmer and more graceful, and the capitals are decorated with scroll-like carvings.

Corinthian columns, which were meant to be like trees, were developed in about 400 BC. The columns are slender and the capitals are deep and decorated with carvings of acanthus leaves. It is rare to see Corinthian capitals in Nabataean art.

The fall of Petra

At the height of its power, Petra would have been bustling with merchants from all over the East. There would have been a busy market where people could meet to trade with each other and exchange news.

By the time of King Aretas III the city would have been like a Roman town with a sacred area or temenos containing a large temple. Petra's great temple, the Kasr el Bint, is one of the few freestanding buildings that survives today. It was built during the reign of King Obdoas II (30–9 BC).

The Nabataeans' independence soon came to an end. The Romans wanted Petra because of its position on the trade routes. By the end of the first century AD the city was surrounded by Roman territory and in AD 106 the Romans took over Petra.

Petra flourished under the Romans, who added new buildings and improved irrigation for farming. But after the Romans had been driven out by invasions from Persia (now Iran) in the third century AD, it became less important and was gradually forgotten.

'A rose-red city'

Petra was rediscovered in 1812 by Jean Louis Burckhardt, a Swiss explorer. He disguised himself as an Arab so that he could travel unnoticed in regions where no Westerner had been before.

Burckhardt wrote a book in which he described the amazing journey along the Siq and the discovery of the rock city. Soon after his book was published, people began to visit Petra. One of these travellers, the artist David Roberts, painted romantic views of the city, from which Dean Burgon wrote the famous line 'A rose-red city, half as old as time'. In fact, the rocks are every other shade of red and pink, except rose!

Alois Musil, an Austrian professor from Prague, carried out the first proper research about Petra and published his findings in 1907. Since then, more detailed archaeological work has been done on the site.

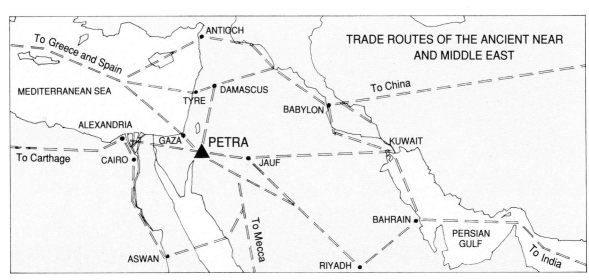

Map showing the many trade routes passing through or near Petra.

Ancient waterworks

Petra was in the desert, where water was in short supply. The Nabataeans needed fresh water, not only for the merchants who passed through, but also for the 20,000 people who lived in Petra. However, the rains did not come often. There would be months of dry weather followed by torrential downpours that turned the rocky pathways into dangerous swirling rivers. The water had to be caught and stored until it was needed.

In order to do this the Nabataeans built a reservoir, Al Birka ('the pool'), in the hills above the city. From this basin, which had a capacity of 2500 cubic metres (88,275 cu. ft), a channel cut through the rock carried water across an aqueduct and down to the city. Here it flowed into another reservoir from which supplies could be drawn. Archaeologists have also found pipes which carried water from springs

A tomb built in the Corinthian style.

directly into the city. Building this system was an incredible achievement, which meant that Petra always had water for travellers and inhabitants alike.

Pots for all

The Nabataeans seem to have been skilled in many ways. Not only did they carve and sculpt Petra out of bare rock and build an efficient water system, but they were also excellent potters. We are not sure where they learned these skills, but it was certainly before the Romans came.

Nabataean kilns filled with pots waiting to be fired have recently been found in Petra. The designs on the pottery are unique but are obviously taken from nature. The thin, delicate china with leaves and branches painted in soft colours have a strangely modern look.

Gods of Petra

The Nabataeans worshipped their own gods but we know little about them. Apart from the kings, two gods have been identified. The principal god of Petra, Dusares, is thought to be the god of the upper classes and is represented by the simple, uncarved blocks of stone which can still be seen in Petra.

The Nabataeans also worshipped the goddess Al Uzza, whom they probably brought with them to Edom. She may have been the goddess of flocks and shepherds.

Alexandria

Egypt, c. 320 BC – AD 391

City of Alexander the Great, of Cleopatra, and of the world's first lighthouse, Alexandria became the greatest seat of learning in the ancient world. But why was its golden age so short-lived?

Many extraordinary people feature in the history of the ancient world, but one man stands out above the others. Alexander the Great was a brilliant leader who devoted his life to conquering lands for Greece. He died when he was only thirty-two, but by then he ruled over an empire that included Greece, Syria, Egypt, Babylonia, Persia and parts of India.

As Alexander conquered new lands, he made them into Greek colonies. The city of Alexandria in Egypt became the centre of the Greek-speaking world. It rose up out of nothing and, in a brief blaze of glory, became a seat of learning and discovery to equal no other. But soon its flame was extinguished for ever.

A new city

Egypt was a mighty kingdom in its own right, but its major cities were in the centre of the country, along the River Nile. Alexander wanted a capital near the Mediterranean so that it would be easier to trade and communicate with other parts of his empire. So he fixed his attention on the coastal town of Rhakotis. This was a fairly small and insignificant Egyptian town, but it did have an excellent natural harbour.

Rhakotis was built on a spur of land which jutted out at the end of the Nile delta. To the south was Lake Mariout, which provided a sheltered mooring for ships. To the north was a long island. Alexander planned to build a causeway linking the island to the spur. This would create new harbours on either side. The island itself was to become the site of the famous lighthouse, one of the Seven Wonders of the Ancient World.

Alexander commissioned the Greek architect Dinocrates to build a his new city. The streets were to be laid out on the grid system, as in

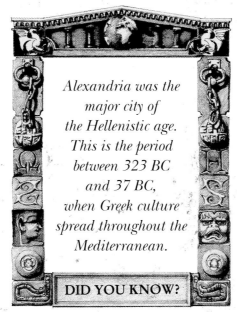

Alexandria was the major city of the Hellenistic age. This is the period between 323 BC and 37 BC, when Greek culture spread throughout the Mediterranean.

DID YOU KNOW?

Alexander the Great broods over his beautiful city and over the famous lighthouse. We have to piece together information about the lighthouse from ancient coins and mosaics. It was built in tiers and the light was a fire burned from the top.

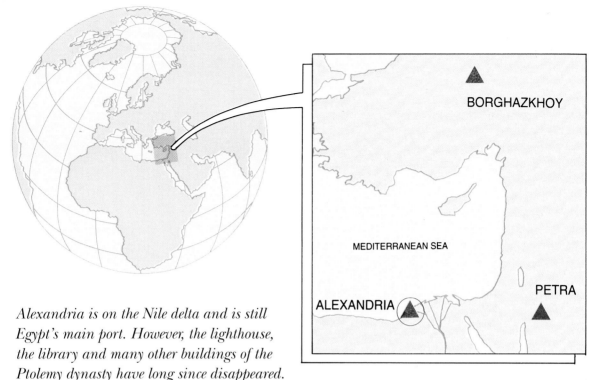

Alexandria is on the Nile delta and is still Egypt's main port. However, the lighthouse, the library and many other buildings of the Ptolemy dynasty have long since disappeared.

the cities of ancient Greece. New harbours were to be created and the buildings were to be decorated in the classical style of Greece.

But Alexander was not to see much of the city he had planned. He set out once again on his conquests and died of a fever in Babylon in 323 BC.

Struggle for power

After Alexander's death, his half-brother, Philip Arrhidaeus, succeeded him as emperor. One of Alexander's generals, Ptolemy, was chosen to govern Egypt. The empire as a whole was still ruled over by the emperor, but this control was weakened when Philip was killed in 317 BC.

As central control grew weaker, so Ptolemy's power in Egypt grew stronger. In the end, it was almost an independent state. Ptolemy made himself king of Egypt in 305 BC, and took the title 'Soter' which means 'saviour'. He was the first of a line of kings which

continued until the death of Cleopatra, the last queen of Egypt, in 30 BC. Egypt was then taken over by the Romans.

But up to that day, Ptolemy and his descendants ruled from Alexandria, which developed into the classical city of Alexander's dreams and became the greatest centre of learning in the ancient world.

The first university

Large parts of the city were built during the reigns of the three kings: Ptolemy I Soter (305–282 BC), Ptolemy II Philadelphus (282–46 BC) and Ptolemy III Euergetes (246–21 BC).

Ptolemy I set up the university complex that was to become such a famous part of Alexandria's history. The complex as a whole was known as the museion. It contained a library, laboratories and lecture halls. Scholars gave lectures, as well as carrying out research, and their subjects could be literary or scientific. Apart from being a university the museion was also a religious centre. It was run by a priest who was chosen by the king.

With this royal interest, its library of books and its scholars, the museion flourished; Alexandria became the intellectual centre of the world. Philosophers came from all over the empire to study there. Scholars studied medicines, maths and the stars.

The city grows

Alexandria was not just a seat of learning. As Alexander had intended, it was a major port and a business centre. The Ptolemies also built a massive palace complex which was almost like a city itself, with temples and government offices alongside the royal apartments.

At first the Egyptians were pushed aside and all the responsible jobs were given to friends and relations of the Ptolemies. The only Egyptians to keep their status were the priests. The Greeks brought their own gods with them, but the Egyptians continued to worship their old gods.

The Egyptians recognised the Ptolemies as their kings, but there were revolts and unrest during the reign of Ptolemy III and his successors.

Gradually, the Egyptians began to take some of the more powerful positions again. By 50 BC the influence of the Greek kings had weakened and the city was divided. It was easy enough for the Romans to take it over. Alexandria's days of glory were finished.

Alexander the Great

Alexander came from Macedonia, a wild and mountainous region to the north of Greece. Macedonia was separate from the city-states of Greece. The people did not all speak Greek and they were ruled by their own king. Alexander's father, Philip of Macedon, became king in 359 BC and set out to conquor Greece. He finally succeeded when he defeated the Greek army at Chaerona in 338 BC.

Alexander the Great.

Alexander had the same aims as his father. He wanted to extend the Greek empire, but he was not just a soldier. During Philip's reign, Athens had remained the centre of Greek culture.

The young Alexander was taught by the Greek philosopher, Aristotle, who gave the boy a love of poetry and art and an interest in science. Greek culture later dominated Alexander's empire.

But Alexander's overriding ambition was to conquer more and more lands. His father had wanted to invade Persia, and this Alexander did. Then he conquered Egypt and Babylon in 331 BC. But his sights were set on India. He crossed the River Indus and conquered the Punjab. He wanted to push on further but his soldiers had had enough, so Alexander turned back. On the way home he caught a fever and died in Babylon in 323 BC.

The harbour and lighthouse

At the time of the Ptolemies, Alexandria was a classical Greek city with many temples and public buildings. Unfortunately, the stretch of water between the mainland and the island had strong currents which were hazardous to shipping. The answer was to build a causeway, known as the heptastadion, linking the city and the island. This divided the stretch of water in two, so reducing the effects of the currents swirling

through, and forming two sheltered harbours. Of course, it also meant that people could cross easily from the mainland to the island.

The eastern harbour was the most important. Some of the palace buildings were at the water's edge, so this also became the harbour for the royal fleet. It was guarded by the great lighthouse, or pharos, which stood at one end of the island. The island was also called Pharos,

which is the Greek word for lighthouse.

The lighthouse was built for two reasons. Firstly, the coastline around the city was treacherous for shipping approaching from the Mediterranean. There were limestone reefs, and rocks at the harbour entrance. The sight of the lighthouse warned sailors that they were approaching this danger zone and its light guided them through to safety.

But the lighthouse had another important function. The city was always under threat of attack from the sea, so the tower served as a look-out where the people could watch for approaching enemies. The island of Pharos had its own small walled town which was separate from the great city across the causeway. Some of its residents probably worked at the lighthouse as mechanics, labourers or look-outs.

'Serpent of the Nile'

Cleopatra (69–30 BC) was the last and probably the best-known queen of Egypt. She first came to the throne in 51 BC and ruled with her brother, Ptolemy XIII. Ptolemy ousted Cleopatra in 48 BC, but by this time the Romans had taken over most of the lands around the Mediterranean. Julius Caesar restored Cleopatra to the throne in 47 BC.

When Caesar was murdered in 44 BC, Mark Antony seized power but was opposed by Caesar's great-nephew Octavian. They divided the empire between them. Antony took over Egypt, where he met and fell in love with Cleopatra in 41 BC. He deserted his wife Octavia, the sister of Octavian, to live in Alexandria with her. This gave Octavian his chance. He waged war on Antony and Cleopatra and defeated their fleet at the Battle of Actium in 31 BC. They both committed suicide in 30 BC, and Octavian became the first Roman emperor, taking the name Augustus.

Queen Cleopatra.

The Pharos

The lighthouse, or pharos, was a unique building which became the symbol of Alexandria. It was destroyed by an earthquake in the fourteenth century, so we have to rely on medieval reports and drawings to tell us what it was like. The strange thing is that the pharos was built on a very grand scale for a lighthouse. It was at least 122 metres (400 ft) high and built of gleaming white limestone or marble.

It was divided into four storeys, each one narrower than the storey below. The lowest storey was a square room where the mechanics and lighthouse-keepers spent their time. A ramp led up to the octagonal second storey. This and the smaller circular third storey above probably only contained ramps leading up to the top of lighthouse. There were windows all round for the look-outs.

The light at the top was created by the flames of a wood fire. During the day, when the flames could not be seen so clearly, smoke from the fire billowed out to signal the position of the pharos. The light was probably directed out to sea by mirrors made of polished metal.

A reconstruction of the pharos.

Alexandria's library

The world-famous library may have contained as many as 700,000 books and papers. The 'books' were written on scrolls of paper made from the papyrus reeds that grew by the River Nile. Scribes made copies of the books as they came in and also kept records of people who borrowed the books, much as librarians do today.

We have to guess about the exact organisation of the library. For example, we do not know if there was a reading room or if people took the books away. There seems to have been one large library where most of the books were kept, and another smaller one, perhaps for the books people consulted most.

There were books on every subject, from science to plays and poetry. Many of the works were in Greek, but literature from Egypt, Persia and the Bible lands was translated and kept there as well.

Ptolemy IV with confiscated scrolls for the library.

The grain bowl of Europe

Egypt was vitally important to its conquerors because of its fertile land beside the River Nile where crops such as wheat could be grown. Egypt was one of the ancient world's main suppliers of grain.

Farmers in ancient Greece grew wheat and barley, but the land was mountainous and the soil dry and poor, so the Greeks needed supplies of grain for themselves and for trading. When Egypt became part of the Greek empire, the Ptolemies and other Greek overlords became wealthy from trading in Egyptian wheat exported from the port of Alexandria.

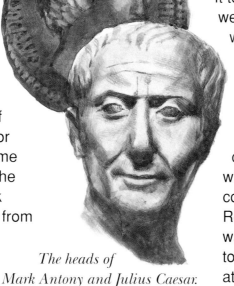

The heads of Mark Antony and Julius Caesar.

Later on, as the Roman empire expanded, the Romans set up a network of trade. Now Roman cargo ships carried wheat from Egypt to feed the common people of Rome. It took two or three weeks for a ship filled with cargo to sail from Egypt to Rome. The Roman populace was fickle and would rebel without their 'bread and circuses', so anyone who controlled Egypt could hold the ruler of Rome to ransom. That was why Octavian had to defeat Mark Antony at all costs.

Where to go

Although pictures will tell you a lot, it's much better to go to a museum and look at all the things that archaeologists have found from a vanished civilisation. You will get an even better idea of how a people lived and worked and what they thought was important by looking at the statues, jewellery, pottery and other remains.

Some museums have special visiting days when they let you actually touch these ancient things and examine them properly. Often school visits are allowed special access to items which are not usually on display if they are studying a particular period or culture. But **always** check the opening days and times before you try to visit a museum to avoid disappointment.

British museums

The following museums have good general collections on display from some of the civilisations featured in this book:

British Museum, Great Russell St, London WC2 (071–636 1555)

Birmingham Museum & Art Gallery, Chamberlaine Sq, Birmingham (021–253 2834)

Fitzwilliam Museum, Trumpington St, Cambridge (0223–332900)

University Museum of Archaeology and Anthropology, Downing St, Cambridge (0223–337733)

Ashmolean Museum, Beaumont St, Oxford (0865–278000)

Pitt-Rivers Museum, South Parks Rd, Oxford (0865–270927)

Royal Museum of Scotland, Queen St, Edinburgh (031–255 7534)

Glasgow Museum & Art Gallery, Kelvingrove, Glasgow (041–357 3929)

The Burrell Collection, Pollok Country Park, Glasgow G43 (041–649 7151)

Specific sites

Ur – the things that Sir Leonard Woolley found were distributed equally between the British Museum in London, the Pennsylvania Museum in Philadelphia, USA and the Bagdad Museum in Bagdad, Iraq.

Saqqara, Karnak, Abu Simbel – there are enormous collections of Ancient Egyptian material in the British Museum in London, the Louvre Museum in Paris, the Museo Egizio in Turin, Italy and the Aegyptische Museum in Berlin. The biggest collection is in the Archaeological Museum in Cairo, Egypt. There you can see the fabulous treasures that came from the tomb of King Tutankhamen.

Babylon – most of the material found by Robert Koldewey is either in the Bagdad Museum or the Vorderasiatisches Museum in Berlin. Material from later excavations is in the Bagdad Museum.

Boghazköy – there is a small museum at Borghazkhöy itself. Other Hittite material is in the Anatolian Civilisations Museum in Ankara and the Museum of the Ancient Orient in Istanbul, Turkey.

Khorsabad – the Bagdad Museum and the British Museum have good collections of Assyrian material.

Persepolis – there is a museum at Persepolis, displaying finds from the excavations. The Archaeological Museum in Tehran also has a fine collection of Persian remains. Other good collections are in the Louvre Museum in Paris and the Metropolitan Museum of Art in New York, USA.

Petra – the best collection of material from the Nabatean civilisation is in the Archaeological Museum in Amman, Jordan.

Alexandria – the Graeco-Roman Museum in Alexandria has the best collection of material from the old city.

Find out some more:

Egypt and Mesopotamia – Unstead, R.J. (A.&C. Black, 1985)

Egyptian Craftsmen – Caselli, Giovanni (Macdonald, 1986)

Everyday Life in Babylonia and Assyria – Saggs, HWF (Dorset Press, 120 Fifth Avenue, New York, NY 10011, USA, 1988)

First Civilisations – Millard, Anne (Usbourne, 1977)

First Empires, The – Rowland-Entwistle, Theodore (Franklin Watts, 1990)

Gods & Pharoahs from Egyptian Mythology – Harris, Geraldine (Peter Lowe, 1982)

Growing up in Ancient Egypt – Ferguson, Sheila (Batsford, 1980)

Mesopotamian Myths – McCall, I. (British Museum Publications, 1990)

Petra – Browning, Iain (Chatto & Windus, 1989)

Tales of Ancient Egypt – Green, Roger Lancelyn (Puffin, 1989)

Some adult books you might enjoy:

Alexandria: a history and a guide – Forster, E.M. (M.Haag, 1986)

Ancient Turkey: a traveller's history of Anatolia – Lloyd, Seton (British Museum Publications, 1989)

Warrior Pharoahs – Newby, P.H. (Faber & Faber, 1980)

Index

Abraham 13
Abu Simbel, Egypt 11, 53–7
Achaemenids (Media) 67–8
Actium, battle of (31 BC) 88
Ahmose, Prince 45
Ahriman (Persian evil spirit) 75
Ahuramazda (Persian supreme god) 75
Akhenaten (Amenhotep IV) 51
Akhetaten, Egypt (Tel el Amarna) 51
Akkad (empire) 14, 61
al Uzza (Nabataean goddess) 81
Alexander the Great, Emperor 73, 74, 83–5
Alexandria, Egypt 11, 83–9
  causeway 86-7
  library 89
  lighthouse 86–8
  palace 85, 86
  university 84–5
Amenhotep III 48
Amenophis III 50
Amitiya, Queen 31, 32, 68
Amun (Egyptian sun god) 45–7, 51, 55
Anatolia (Turkey) 14, 37–43
Annunaki (Babylonian judges of hell) 31
Anubis (Egyptian death god) 23
Apsu (ocean god) 31
Arbela, Iraq 59
Aretas III, King 79, 80
Aristotle (philosopher) 85
army 65
Artaxerxes, King 69, 73
Arzawa, Turkey 43
Ashur, Tab-shar (Assyrian architect) 60
Assur, Iraq 15, 59, 60
Assurbanipal, King 65
Assyrians 10, 29, 31, 39, 42, 43, 59–65
Aswan Dam, Egypt 27, 57
Aten (Egyptian god) 51
Athens, Greece 73, 73, 85

Babel, Tower of 29, 34
Babylon, Iraq 10, 29–35, 67, 68, 73, 85
  Hanging Gardens 32
  walls 34
Babylonian Empire 30, 60, 72, 83
Boghazköy, Turkey 10, 11, 37–43
Botta, Paul Emile 65

bricks 15, 16–17
Burckhardt, Jean Louis 80
Burgon, Dean 80
burial ritual 18, 21–3
Byron, Lord (English poet) 61

Cambyses, King 68
Chaerona, battle of (338 BC) 85
chariots
  Assyrian 59, 65
  Hittite 36
Chevrier, Henri 51
Chicago University 65
classes, of people 30, 38–9
Cleopatra, Queen 84, 88
coronation, Egyptian 23
Cyaxerxes, King 68
Cyprus 43
Cyrus the Great, King 31, 68, 75

Darius, King 67–9, 72, 74
Darius III, King 73, 74
Delian League (Greece) 73
Dinocrates (architect) 83
Dur Sharrukin see Khorsabad
Dusares (Nabatean god) 81

Ea (Mesopotamian god of wisdom) 31, 39, 64
Edom 77
Egypt 10, 21–7, 42 45–51, 53–7, 67, 68, 72, 83, 85
  Middle Kingdom 45, 47
  New Kingdom 45–6, 47
  Upper & Lower 23, 26, 35
Enkidu (companion of Gilgamesh) 64
Enlil (Mesopotamian storm god) 64
Eretria, Greece 72
Euphrates river 10, 13–15, 19, 43, 59
Exodus (Bible) 10

farming 10, 13–15, 27, 38, 54, 59, 89

Gasga people 39, 42
Genesis (Bible) 13
Gilgamesh, legendary king 63, 64
  Epic of 64, 65
government, system of 26, 61
grave goods 13, 18–19, 22
Greece 11, 72–3, 83–5
Gutians 14

Hammurabi, King 29-30
Hanging Gardens, Babylon 32
Hattusas 37
Hattusilis I (or Labarnas), King 37, 43
Hattusilis III, King 42
Haxamanish (or Achaemenes), King 67
headdresses 18
Hebat (Hittite sun goddess) 39
Herodotus (Greek historian) 34
Hittites 10, 37–43
Horemheb, King 53
Horus (Egyptian sun god) 25, 55, 56
Hrihor (high priest of Amun) 47
Hyksos people 45

Imhotep (Egyptian architect) 20, 21–2, 26
India 67, 68, 83, 85
Iran 15, 67–75
Iraq, 13–19, 29–35, 59–65
Ishtar (Babylonian love/war goddess) 35, 61
  Gate, Babylon 34
Isis (Egyptian love goddess) 55, 56
Israel 10
Issus, battle of (333 BC) 73

jewellery 14, 18–19
Jews 10, 29, 31, 68
Jordan 11, 45, 77–81
jubilee (of Egyptian kings) 23, 25
Judah (Palestine) 29
Julius Caesar 88

Kalhu, Iraq 60
Karnak, Egypt 10, 45–51
  Great Hypostyle Hall 45, 46, 48
Khorsabad, Turkey 10, 59–65
  palace 61–3
Kish, King of 64
Koldewey, Robert 34
Kumarbi (Hittite god) 39
Kushites 47

Labarnas see Hattusilis I
Lacau, Pierre 51
laws 29–30, 35, 39, 43
Lebanon 45
Legrain, Georges 51
Libya 47, 68

lighthouse, Alexandria 86–8

Macedonia 85
Makridi, Dr Theodore 43
Marathon, battle of (490 BC) 72
Marduk (Babylonian storm god)
    31
    temple of 34
Mariette, Auguste 27
Mariout, Lake 83
Mark Antony 88
Medes 31, 67–8
Menes, King of Nekhem 26
Mesopotamia 10, 13–19, 29–35,
    59–65
metalworking 19, 43, 60
mummification 23
Mummu (Babylonian god) 31
Musil, Alois 80
Mut (Egyptian goddess) 55
Muttwallis, King 42

Nabataeans 77–81
Nabonicus, King 31
Nabopolassar, King 31
Nanna (Sumerian moon god)
    15
Nebuchadnezzar, King 29, 31,
    68
Nekhen, Egypt 21, 26
Nile river 21, 26, 27, 53, 57, 83
Nineveh, Iraq 59, 60, 61, 68
Ningal (Sumerian goddess) 15
Ninmar (Babylonian birth
    goddess) 34
Nofretari, Queen 54, 55
Nubia 47, 53–4, 56

Obdoas II, King 80
Octavia, wife of Mark Antony
    88
Octavian (Emperor Augustus)
    88, 89
Osiris (Egyptian god of the
    dead) 55, 56

palaces, Alexandria 85, 86
    Khorsabad 61, 62–4
    Persepolis 67–9, 73
Palestine 68
Persepolis 11, 67–75
    New Year celebrations 69, 70
    palace 67–9, 73
Persia 10, 31, 67–75, 83, 85
Petra, Jordan 11, 77–81
    Kasr el Bint temple 80
    Khasneh (treasury) 76, 79

pharoahs 10, 21–3, 45–7, 50,
    52–6
    see also individual headings
Philip Arrhidaeus, Emperor 84
Philip of Macedon, King 85
Place, Victor 65
Plataea, battle of (479 BC) 73
pottery, Nabataean 81
Ptah (Egyptian craftsmen's god)
    55
Ptolemy I Soter 84–5
Ptolemy II Philadelphus 84–5
Ptolemy III Euergetes 84–5
Ptolemy IV 89
Ptolemy XIII 88
Puduhepa, Queen 42
pyramids, Giza 21
    Saqqara 11, 20, 24–5, 27
    see also ziggurats

Qadesh, battle of (c.1286 BC)
    42, 46, 55

Ra (or Re), (Egyptian sun god)
    25, 56
Rameses I 46, 53
Rameses II 42, 46, 48
Rameses III 47
Re-Harakhty (Egyptian sun god)
    55, 56
Rhakotis, Egypt 83
road-building 68, 69
Roberts, David 80
Romans 80, 84, 85, 88, 89
Roxane, wife of Alexander 74

Salamis, battle of (480 BC) 73
Sameth (Babylonian justice god)
    35
Saqqara, Egypt 11, 21–7
    step pyramids 11, 20, 24–5,
    27
Sardis, Turkey 69
Sargon, King of Akkad 14, 60 61
Sargon II 59–61, 65
seals 19
Sennacherib, King 61
Senwosret, King 46
Set (Egyptian night god) 56
Seti I 46, 53, 56
Siq, gorge of (Jordan) 78–9
slaves 30, 38, 56
Sparta, Greece 72, 73
Sumerian Empire 13, 14
    civilisation 13–19
Susa, Iran 15, 67–9, 73
Syria 37, 45, 60, 83

taxation 26, 59, 74, 78
Tel el Amarna see Akhetaten
Telepinus, King 42
tels (mounds over buried cities)
    34, 65
temples, Babylonian 34, 60
    Egyptian 10, 44, 45, 46, 48, 52,
    57
    Nabataean 80
    see also ziggurats
Teshub (Hittite weather god) 39
Texier, Charles 43
Thebes, Egypt 45, 47, 55
Themistocles (Greek general)
    72–3
Thermopylae, battle of (480
    BC) 72
Tiammat (Babylonian chaos
    goddess) 31
Tiglath-pileser I, King 59
Tiglath-pileser II, King 59–60
Tigris river 10, 13, 15, 59
tombs 14, 18–19, 20, 21–2, 24–5,
    79, 81
trade 19, 67, 69, 77–8, 80, 90
Tudhiliyas IV, King 43
Turkey 14, 37–43
Tutankhamun, King 51
Tuthmosis III, King 48, 50

university of Alexandria 84–5
Ur, Iraq 10, 13–19, 59
    ziggurat 13–15, 16–17, 21
Ur-Nammu, King 14–15
Uruk, Iraq 15, 64
Utnapishtim (demi-god, see
    Gilgamesh) 64

Valley of the Queens, Thebes 55
Vishtaspa, King 75

wall paintings 23, 26, 56
waterworks 26, 27, 32, 56, 81
weapons 14, 43
Winkler, Dr Hugo 43
Woolley, Sir Leonard 18
worship ritual 50
writing, cuneiform 13, 15, 19,
    21, 29, 43, 74

Xerxes, King 69, 72–3

ziggurats 13, 30, 31
    at Ur 13–15, 16-17, 21
Zoroaster (religious leader) 75
Zoroastrianism 67, 74
Zoser, King 21–3, 25